MEDITATING ON THE PSALMS

D0873661

MEDITATING ON THE PSALMS

JOHN EATON

WESTMINSTER
JOHN KNOX PRESS
LOUISVILLE · KENTUCKY

© 2004 Continuum Publishing

This edition of this work is published by arrangement with Continuum
International Publishing Group Ltd.

All rights reserved. No part of this book may be reproduced or transmitted in any
form or by any means, electronic or mechanical, including photocopying, recording,
or by any information storage or retrieval system, without permission in writing
from the publisher. For information, address Westminster John Knox Press, 100
Witherspoon Street, Louisville, Kentucky 40202-1396.

Published in the United States by Westminster John Knox Press, Louisville,
Kentucky.

Published in Great Britain by Continuum Publishing.

Cover design by Pam Poll.
Typeset by Tradespools, Frome, Somerset.
Printed and bound in Great Britain by Cromwell Press.

04 05 06 07 08 09 10 11 12 13 - 10 9 8 7 6 5 4 3 2 1

Library of Congress Cataloging-in-Publication Data is on file at the
Library of Congress, Washington, D.C.

ISBN 0-664-22930-1

⤲ *Contents* ⤲

❧ Preface ❧

Most people have encountered a psalm, if only at a funeral. And many people again have heard or sung psalms quite often, but without experiencing their power. Might the psalms presented in this book, along with the interpretations I have offered, give the opportunity for a great discovery?

One psalmist had noticed a swallow nesting in some high crevice of the temple court. With what eagerness, what confidence she kept flying in to her home near the Lord's altar! It was a parable of the pilgrim-soul finding, after a hard journey, peace and new life in the nearness to God. Can the little bird be also a parable for our pilgrimage though the psalms? Can we look and listen, commit mind and heart to the quest, until we too find in the sanctuary of the psalms that home near to God where we shall come often and with delight?

But how to enter the psalms' world of meditation and vision? It is quite a good plan to work with a selection of the hundred and fifty poems. I have chosen fifty-two, convenient for a steady and thoughtful progress through the weeks of the year. I have drawn the translation and interpretation from my recent large work, *The Psalms: a Historical and Spiritual Commentary* (T&T Clark 2003). By omitting complications of detail, I have aimed at an unbroken flow, heightening the meaning for today. Some readers, perhaps group-leaders especially, will still be glad to follow up issues of translation and understanding in the longer book.

A good time to begin such a pilgrimage of the soul is the season of Lent. Some psalms in my selection are rich in Lenten themes – penitence in 51, God's deep knowing of us in 139, the fleeting nature of earthly life in 39 and 90, the yearning for renewal in 42–3 and 126. But all the psalms are as relevant to Lent as Lent is to every day of our life: Lent, the time of lengthening light and the greening of spring, and of hearts renewed in communion with the living Creator. And all the psalms contribute to the opportunity of every day, the 'today' when they would have us hear his voice and not harden our hearts; meditate in stillness, turn to him in trust and entreaty and thanksgiving. Daily the psalms can bring us vision of the divine strength, care and purpose that tower above the human hurryings and scurryings. And all in company with the countless host of other psalm-pilgrims and in fellowship with all the creatures of God.

I am grateful to the people at T&T Clark International for proposing and seeing through this work; I have found them dynamic, positive and kind. Then there are those who have supported me with love and prayer, some sharing my pilgrimage by daily using my large commentary, offering comments from time to time (you especially, Keith). Also, since the death of my two dear cats Thomasina and Talitha, I have been touched by the friendship of a number of birds in the garden, not least Thora the thrush who eats from my hand, Bronwen the bossy blackbird, and Charles the well-dressed raven; also by Klaus and Violet, two young visiting cats, brother and sister, red tabbies with yellow collars, as pretty as pretty could be. The psalms bind us all together, and with earth, sea and sky. But I dedicate the book to the one who is constantly with me and has so often saved the day – my beloved wife Margaret.

John Eaton

❦ *Introduction* ❦

A first encounter

There can't be many Iron Age songs still in constant use today. The Hebrew songs known as Psalms, dating from about 1000–400 BCE, are not only still in use, but are also found to be of great spiritual value. On the page they stand as a collection of one hundred and fifty poems, and you would be hard put to it to find a language they have not been translated into.

They have been the most used part of the Bible. Uncannily, they have seemed to turn the Christian gospel into music, and beyond all other compositions have given expression to prayers without number. All down the centuries and to this day, they have fostered communion with God. Before the Holy One, infinite and eternal, when mouths and hearts might have been closed through ignorance or former alienation, the Psalms have enabled people to speak and to listen, to be at home in the practice of prayer and praise, and so to know the Lord.

From ancient times, especially when a group worshipped together, poetry and music were like angels carrying words to and from heaven. They were the bearers of intense feelings and of inspiration. And so it is that the psalm prayers, praises and divine messages took the form of songs: poetry to be chanted to the accompaniment of musical instruments. That is what 'psalm' meant – such a sacred song aided especially by the plucked strings of lyre or harp. Our collection was gathered chiefly from worship at the temple in Jerusalem. And amazingly, it has continued to be at the core of worship in the spiritual Jerusalem, the abiding sanctuary where all may meet with their Creator and Lord.

The Psalms as poems

The great European poets seem virtually killed by translation. The subtlety and beauty of their masterpieces are drained out. A close translation sounds flat, and sometimes even ridiculous. So how could this Hebrew poetry have survived translation? How could it retain its beauty and power when transformed into every language under the sun?

It was because the Hebrew poets composed in a style which in important respects can survive, even flourish, in translation. The essential feature of this translatable style is that its patterns are woven more in sense than in sound. Rhythm and word-music are used, but more important is the weaving of sense; and that is something which can be reproduced fairly well in translation. If you look at my translation of Psalm 8.6–8, you will see that each verse has two parts which match each other, saying almost the same thing. It is the method of 'parallelism'. Lest it should become monotonous, the poets varied it skilfully. Thus in Psalm 67 you will notice that verses 1, 2, 3, 5 and 6 have two such closely parallel parts, but verse 4 has three; verse 7 appears to be in two parts, but in reality has just one statement running right through, so accelerating the tempo of thought. These are simple variations. Other psalms use subtler patterns, sometimes known to be very ancient – so 29.3–5 and 93.3–4. And the beauty of it is that all such effects – simplicity, balance, emphasis, lingering, accelerating – can be caught more or less in any other language.

The Hebrew poets have also obliged us by using plain and unpretentious wording, generally the language of common speech. It is not larded with adjectives or spun out into long, complicated sentences. It hardly ever uses rhyme, and the metre of the lines seems rather loose and variable. There can be play on the sound of words (as strikingly in 122.6), but this is not so common.

Much study has been devoted to the various forms or types into which the psalms can be sorted. You have only to read a few psalms to become aware of such different types. Psalm 1 is a kind of teaching, addressed to those who would be disciples of the Lord; this is often called 'a Wisdom psalm'. Psalm 8, on the other hand, is addressed to the Lord, a praise expressive of awe, wonder and gratitude – usually called 'a hymn'. Psalms 39 and 88 are prayers from someone in distress – often called 'individual laments'. Psalm 74 is the prayer of the nation in trouble – 'a communal lament'. Psalm 45 is for a royal wedding, Psalm 72 for an enthronement – hence 'royal (ceremonial) psalms'. We easily notice such different types, and begin to see how the characteristics of each psalm reflect its aim and setting.

But here we have to take account of tradition and custom. For each particular setting and purpose there developed customary thoughts and expressions. So a lamenting psalm would very likely invoke the name of God, beg for a hearing, describe the distress and the danger from enemies, plead loyalty and trust, promise thank-offerings and testimony of praise when saved. Or a hymn most commonly would summon other worshippers, peoples, indeed all creatures, to praise God; and then it would follow up such calls with reasons, stating that God is praiseworthy as Creator, deliverer, powerful, faithful, merciful.

Such combining of thoughts became traditional building blocks in the various kinds of psalm. Study of them helps greatly with the overall interpretation. Nevertheless, sameness did not oppress the psalms. Poetic inspiration flourished, a fresh fountain. The customary wording and clusters of ideas were like a spring-board for leaps of beauty and intense feeling. We find that almost every psalm has poetic and spiritual treasure of its own.

Every now and then you come across an 'alphabetic' or 'acrostic' psalm. Psalm 25 is an example in our selection. In such psalms the verses begin with successive letters of the Hebrew alphabet – not so much for purposes of memorization as for an ideal of wholeness and order. Here the poet felt the help of a hallowed framework, and could do something of special skill and fullness for the Lord. To modern critics this alphabetic poetry has seemed rather fragmented and forced. But to those who will meditate, the verses often appear as independent short poems of the spirit, with a vast depth beneath their apparent simplicity.

The Psalms as songs

Still today, traditional singing in Asia and Africa often takes the form of an interchange between a soloist and a group, who provoke and encourage each other. Many a heavy task seems lighter when the people at work sing together. The soloist takes the main part of the song, often calling to the others. The group respond with short phrases, probably a repeated refrain.

In the Psalms the signs are again that the main part was carried by a solo singer. In the psalms of praise, this leader often calls to the mass of worshippers, prompting them to utter together short phrases such as 'His faithfulness is for ever', 'Blessed be the Lord', or just 'Amen and amen'. Happy those, it was said, who experienced those festal shouts (89.15)!

However, there were also skilled choirs of singers, and their parts seem to be preserved in some psalms, such as the opening and closing verses of Psalm 8. Psalm 27 seems to close with a comforting word from the choir to the soloist: 'Wait for the Lord, be strong and let your heart take courage; yes, wait in hope for the Lord.' As the use of underlying drone notes on instruments was common, it is quite possible that the choirs also sang those droning underlays which we hear today so powerfully from Russian or South African choirs.

The singing was rendered with intense emotion. There was a sharp difference in style between praises and laments. The praises expressed high joy, supported by rhythmic clapping and dancing. The laments might also be loud, and were said to resemble the moaning of doves or the groaning of bears. On one occasion (so Ezra 3.10f) the order was for praise, with cymbals, trumpets and acclamations. But there arose also from some of the people a spontaneous wailing of lament. The combined noise carried far across the hills.

But we must not imagine that the worship was *all* very noisy. The loud praises echoed in the psalms, with all that clapping and dancing, belonged to the high moments in the long pilgrimage festivals. Psalms 62 and 65 show how stillness before God was valued. There was sometimes a music of hushed awe and a praying of silent trust.

Highly esteemed were the musical instruments. Sometimes called 'instruments of song', they were closely united with the voices before God. As in oriental styles still today, they might play in unison with the singer, adding their emotional colours. They would also accentuate the rhythm and add introductions, interludes, and conclusions. The main-stay was the plucked-string music of lyres and harps, but there were also pipes (kinds of flutes, clarinets and oboes), trumpets (animal horns or silver), and a good range of percussion – hand-drums (some like tambourines), shakers and clackers. The extensive use of such instruments in sung worship is confirmed by the story of David's founding act, when he installed the ark in Jerusalem (2 Samuel 6), and also by the fact that the last psalm in the collection, the last word in temple praise, devotes such a large proportion of its words to mention of musical instruments (Psalm 150).

In the music of praise there was a joining with all the voices of God's creatures – all peoples and what we call 'the natural world', a universal music of worship and gratitude to God. The heart of all the singing was the calling of the name of God. Here music found its full meaning as experience of his presence, as communion with him so graciously revealed: 'My glory and my music is the Lord' (118.14).

Scarcely understood is the frequent notice in the psalms usually rendered 'Pause' (Psalm 24 etc.). It may have signalled an interlude for instrumental music or for a general bowing down with words of reverence.

Authors and singers of the Psalms

The psalms have traditionally been credited to David. By New Testament times it was customary to speak of him as the author, though this was really a kind of shorthand, for Jewish scholars recognized that others had also contributed. A number of names indeed appear in the headings over the Hebrew of the psalms, though David's name is by far the most frequent (73 times). The expression ('Of David') in question, however, may not have been intended to establish the authorship. 'Of' might have meant 'Pertaining to', and 'David' might mean his dynasty.

When modern scholars came to think of most of the psalms as being much later than David's time, opinion hardened against the possibility of his authorship. But the question has seemed more open again, as the dating has been reconsidered and often pushed back towards the great early days of the monarchy.

Certainly, David was portrayed in national tradition as a gifted musician and poet – 'the sweetest singer of Israel' (2 Samuel 23.1). He could well have composed and sung psalms, though it is hard to prove particular examples (23, 51, 71 are sometimes advocated). Most of the composing and performing and the careful handing down of the tradition was probably the work of the family guilds serving the temple, such as are mentioned in some psalm headings and especially in the Books of Chronicles (1 Chronicles 15, 16, 25). It is said in Chronicles that these guild-musicians 'prophesied' – uttered inspired compositions – under the direction of the king. All in all, we can well see David as the father of our Book of Psalms, if only through his work of making Jerusalem the national centre of worship in 1000 BCE and founding the system and institutions of worship there.

The custom of later times in speaking sweepingly of the psalms as uttered by David through the spirit of prophecy has its value. It rightly makes a special link with the Davidic house, the temple and the foreshadowing of the royal

Messiah. And it also recognizes the reach of the psalms far beyond their original situations. Through their music and poetry, their prayer and spiritual communion, they penetrated to a level of truth which made them 'prophecy', reflections of the purpose and work of God.

Psalms in ceremonies of worship

From Jewish tradition and from the character of many psalms we see that Jerusalem's pilgrimage festivals were of major importance for psalm-singing. Granted that psalms might be used in other times of worship – daily offerings, sabbaths, new moons, specially convened fast-days – yet in the collection handed down to us much relates to the festivals.

The chief national festival for the period of the kings, and several centuries before and after, was not the Passover, but the holy season about the time of the autumnal new year. It was often called just 'the pilgrimage of the Lord' or 'the Feast' (*ḥag*). The season will have included days which were later picked out as New Year's Day, Day of Atonement, and week of Tabernacles (1, 10, and 15–22 of the autumn month Tishri, meaning 'Beginning'). This pilgrimage was of tremendous importance for the life and faith of the people, as we shall see in Psalms 84 and 122. Its rich meaning will strike us as we ponder such psalms as 24, 29, 65, 93 and 95.

Outside the calendar of worship, there are many psalms that arise from times of danger or suffering. The particulars given remain rather general and in customary phrases. Scholars have suggested various settings, such as when decisions were given at the temple about accused persons or asylum seekers (hence themes of justice or shelter). It may be best, however, as in the present work, to keep close to tradition and see the prayer often as that of a king (David or his successors). We then appreciate why so much of the distress involves fierce enemies (including armies and nations), imagery of battle, and reference to God's special promises, and also why the psalm can move easily between the semblance of an individual's prayer and the drawing-in of the whole people, for the king is both an individual and a representative. We have to remember that, unlike modern societies, the ancient peoples understood their politics in a strong religious light. It was normal for the deepest and tenderest expressions of relation to God to be made in the prayers and thanksgivings of kings.

Singing through the storms of history

It is helpful to keep in mind some events of history that influenced the psalms. While singing in worship must go back to time immemorial, one historical event was of special importance for the rise of the tradition that gave us our psalms. This was King David's capture of Jerusalem in 1000 BCE. The ancient Canaanite city now became his capital. Skilled people from the native population entered his service, including musicians and singers. The decisive act was his bringing the ark of the Lord to rest in Jerusalem (2 Samuel 6), giving the city pre-eminence as the centre of worship for his great empire. The ark will have stood in some kind of sanctuary called 'the house of the Lord' (2 Samuel 12.20). David had 'found a place for the Lord' (Psalm 132.5, 7). Here the king will have established the orders and duties of priests and psalmists as tradition recounted. Here too he could pour out his own songs to God as he felt moved to do so.

With the peace and prosperity of his son Solomon's reign (970–931 BCE), it was possible to build the famous temple on the higher hill immediately north of the old city. Psalm poetry and music will have been of a standard to match the fine architecture. The tradition David had established entered a golden period.

Though the empire split after the death of Solomon, Jerusalem was still able to continue for three and a half centuries as the seat of the Davidic dynasty. It was still seen as the Lord's throne-centre. The northern tribes had their own kingdom and sanctuaries, such as Bethel and Dan. It may be that some of their psalms found their way to Jerusalem when the northern kingdom was crushed by the Assyrians (from northern Iraq, 721 BCE). Still, the psalm tradition of Jerusalem upheld its faith that the Lord's rule was mediated through the house of David and Jerusalem.

An era ended when the Babylonians (from southern Iraq) destroyed the temple and put an end to David's kingdom (587 BCE). But during the desolate half-century that followed, the lamenting worship was still offered on the ruined site of the temple (Psalm 74), while in Babylonia Jewish exiles commemorated Zion's tragedy and maintained their tradition (Psalm 137). With the establishment of the Persian empire (539 BCE), the exiles could begin to return and the temple be rebuilt. It was dedicated in 515 BCE. Although not as fine as Solomon's temple, it was able to continue as the heart of Hebrew worship for nearly six centuries. When the city walls were restored, psalmists led thanksgiving with cymbals, harps, lyres, trumpets and all the musical instruments 'of David, the man of God' (Nehemiah 12.27–43).

Greek empires succeeded the Persian (from 333 BCE). Later, after a short period of independence under a Jewish priestly family (the Hasmoneans or 'Maccabees'), the country passed into Roman control (64 BCE). Rome sanctioned the reign of Herod (who was part Jewish, part Edomite) from 40–4 BCE. He undertook a massive reconstruction of the temple and its courts. It was a glorious sanctuary throughout the time of Jesus and Paul. But its end was near. In a war of rebellion against Rome, temple and city were destroyed, and Jews banned from the area (70 CE). The guilds of psalmists, with the knowledge and skill of their tradition, vanished from the scene of history. Yet, as now part of scripture and planted in many a pious heart, the psalms lived on.

Psalm landscape

Jerusalem is one of several famous biblical towns situated along the high watershed that runs north to south through Palestine. The mountains, 2000 or 3000 feet high, prevail in this heartland of the psalms. Their western slopes have the better rainfall and green growth. Their arid eastern sides crumple steeply down into the deep trough of the Jordan valley and Dead Sea, far below sea level, and form an inhospitable wilderness.

The fertile areas seem all the more delightful for the contrast. Wild flowers in their season, fig and olive trees, vines and corn abound. The regular drought from May to October, however, might sometimes be prolonged. The rains of winter might fail, causing starvation. Streams and springs in any case were sparse, and water had to be stored in cisterns cut deep into the rock beneath the towns. In the far north of the country there was the great massif of Hermon in view, some 9000 feet high, a sight to behold. Snow abounded on the summits, and from its melting cascades the River Jordan took its rise. The river passed south into the lake of Galilee, then down, down through scrubby jungle into the great salt-lake of the Dead Sea.

These features form the landscape of the psalmists. True, there are also references to seas, islands and ships, but these are usually part of a symbolic poetry descended from more ancient coastal peoples, especially from Lebanon. Most characteristic for the psalms are the mountains, the lovely stretches and pockets of fertility, and the harsh and craggy wilderness. The mountains and deserts gave valuable protection from invaders, but because Palestine was a vital bridge between Asia, Africa and Europe, it could not in the end escape the ravages of the imperial armies.

The terrain provided imagery and colour to the poet-singers. We hear of the cliffs and crags of the wilderness, the rock-doves and griffon-vultures or eagles, the nimble rock-hyraxes, wild goats and deer and asses, snakes, lions, bears, foxes, jackals. We relish the fertile places, hills that give good crops and fruit. We see the threat of invasion and at last the catastrophes of destroying armies. We hear the prayers for rescue from the abyss of suffering in famine, war and sickness. And we admire the brave hope of renewal, when the Lord will send his Spirit to give laughter, dreamlike joy, the great turning, as when water comes to the gullies of the wilderness (104.30; 126).

The Psalms among the nations

The psalm-poetry had meaning to unfold as the centuries went by. Take Psalm 30: it appears to have begun as some individual's thanksgiving when healed and brought from mourning to dancing. Yet it acquired a heading 'For the dedication of the house', was used at the offering of first-fruits, and again at the re-dedication of the temple. The psalms in fact proved able to be eloquent in many changing situations. Justice is best done to their power and beauty when the original aim is respected, while at the same time the user comes to meet them – comes with needs and feelings of a later age, which the psalm will connect with and illuminate. The psalm lives, we might say, as it unites with a sympathetic spirit.

In the century or so before the events of the New Testament, the psalms were very much alive. The community settled by the Dead Sea, whose manuscripts have been so marvellously discovered, used psalms abundantly, and found them applying to their own situation. The prophetic force of psalms was also important for other Jewish circles, who found in them word of the coming kingdom of the Lord and his Messiah.

Likewise for Jesus and the early Christians, the psalms were prophecy of burning relevance. They are quoted in the New Testament more than any other book of scripture. As the Gospels unfold their story of Jesus, references to psalms signal the depth of meaning in the events, linking them to an ancient purpose of God. Peter described David as a prophet through whom God by the Holy Spirit had given words concerning Jesus the Messiah (Acts 2.30–1; 4.25).

This interpretation lay at the heart of the prolific use of the psalms in subsequent worship. John Chrysostom ('the Golden-mouthed', bishop of Constantinople and a great preacher on psalms, 347–407 CE) said that in all kinds of worship 'David is first, midst and last' – in church, at home, in the forum, in monasteries, or in the desert. And this pre-eminence of psalms in Christian worship continued through the Middle Ages, with the interpretation still centring on Christ. In the monasteries especially, numerous psalms resounded throughout the day at the set times of prayer.

In the Reformation too, psalms remained very important for piety, morals and doctrine. Luther often preached on them and Calvin wrote a good commentary. Nearer our time, psalms were read especially with appreciation of their poetic expression of individual feeling. No wonder that Psalm 23 was probably the most valued of all, bringing its comfort in the valley of death's shadow.

Today in much Christian worship they have been somewhat overtaken by a huge treasury of modern hymns and choruses. These often draw on psalms, but may seem easier to understand and sing, pleasant in sound and content. The psalms, however, as songs from scripture, so much used by Jesus, the apostles and martyrs and countless worshippers through the many centuries – the psalms are still a unique treasure of communion with God, essentially at home in today's world. They are still able to open the eyes of our spirits to the wonders of his kingdom and of his Christ.

Difficulties and encouragements

Songs from the Middle East's Iron Age are bound to contain some obscurities for people today. Who is this Og, king of Bashan (135.1)? Where are Meribah and Massah (95.8)? To what purport does God want Moab as his wash-pot (60.8)?

What does it mean that he crushed the heads of Leviathan (74.14)? The encouraging thing here is that such obscurities are remarkably few, and those there are can easily be clarified by a commentary. The quaint details can even speak memorably to our own situations – we may need divine help to cope with an Og, to get through our Meribah or Massah, places of Quarrelling and Testing. And have we not met Leviathan, the monster of chaos?

Another difficulty is the frequency of complaint about enemies. The singer seems to have so many determined to harm him, so many that would be overjoyed at his demise. They are for ever hurling words as weapons and laying traps and ambushes. And he himself sometimes replies with prayer and wishes that may seem too violent. No doubt anyone holding high office will sympathize. Many a bishop or prime-minister will have known such unrelenting malice, and perhaps found more comfort in the psalms than in our blander hymns. And then, the enemies are especially the affliction of the royal psalmist, foreshadowing the haters of the Messiah, the Christ. So we are drawn here into the anguish of Christ's passion. By his example we learn to pray for the end of the cruel *as such*, and their rebirth in the divine love.

A deep difficulty may be found in passages which take death to be the end of life and communion with God (Psalms 30, 88, 90). It was a fairly general outlook for the Old Testament people, though not entirely so (as we may find in Psalms 16, 73, 139). But that sad realism bred a great appreciation of the present communion with God. To know him and his faithful love was better than life itself (so 63.3). These people of such short lives entered so deeply into knowledge of this faithful love that they passed it down to us as the key to the mystery. God the faithful one would not forsake the living or the dead (Ruth 2.20). That faithful love and truth came to us in Jesus, and by his rising again it was shown that not even death could defeat the enduring love which is for all his creatures (33.5; 36.5–6). So the psalms were sung gladly in the church of the risen Lord, their deeper truth now shining through.

The psalms share the difficulty of all the Bible, that the ideas about the world's structure are pre-scientific – the earth fixed on waters, sky as a solid arch containing sun, moon and stars and undergirding heavenly waters and regions. We have to take all this poetically, looking for the meaning which this picture-language symbolizes. How much we then receive – an apprehension of God's supremacy, his humility (Psalm 113), the thread of his purpose through all existence, and the particularity of his care and love (Psalm 8)! The psalms after all are music and poetry; they can tell us truth which eludes the natural sciences.

Then there is the difficulty of a kind of favouritism – the idea that one nation should be 'God's people' and one city singled out as loved by God above all others. This, however, is a language unfolding God's purpose. A person, people or city may be chosen and beloved to serve his plan for all, a heavy responsibility. As we see in Psalm 114, the purpose was to benefit all God's world. The chosen city was the place from which God's light was to shine on all; the chosen people were like a priesthood serving to mediate between the mysterious Holy One and all peoples. And in fact the psalms are remarkable for their strongly universal outlook. The vocations of Israel and Jerusalem are not ignored, but many are the passages which see the Lord as the Most High, maker and carer of all, worshipped by a vast congregation of all creatures in the cosmos.

Finally, there is the difficulty of God being described in crudely human form. The singer cries loudly the better to be heard, and asks God to turn his ear. He asks why God has kept his hand at rest in the fold of his garment. God is said to sit, laugh, even fly on the wings of the wind; he keeps our tears in a bottle. There are many such expressions. This very Hebrew way of speaking of God was found difficult in the Greek world long before the New Testament. It has generally been explained as a language to help us have some knowledge of one who is beyond all our understanding. Better than some abstract way of speaking, unnatural to most people, the psalms give us a close involvement with God and his work. They are none the less deep for being simple. They are indeed childlike in expression. But that proves to be their strength, as we turn and become as little children in order to enter the kingdom of God (Psalm 131; Matthew 18.3). And the Bible after all had a tradition that mankind was made in the likeness of God. In picturing God in human terms, the psalmist was helping to prepare for the Word's becoming flesh (John 1.14).

❦ Psalm 1 ❦

The Secret of Happiness

1   *Happy the one who does not walk*
in the counsel of the wicked,
or stand in the way of sinners,
or sit in the circle of the scoffers,
2   *but whose delight is in the teaching of the Lord,*
meditating in his teaching day and night.
3   *Such a one shall be like a tree*
well planted by channels of water,
giving its fruit at its proper time, its leaves never withering –
yes, all this person does shall be fruitful.
4   *Not so the wicked,*
for they are like chaff which the wind drives away.
5   *Therefore the wicked shall not stand in the judgement,*
nor sinners in the assembly of the just.
6   *For the Lord knows the way of the just,*
but the way of the wicked shall come to nothing.

❦

Unlike most psalms, this simple but effective poem is not prayer, praise or oracle, but teaching. The style is like that of the wise, the sages who would hold up an ideal and warn against evil ways. The images of the watered tree and the two ways that part to opposite directions are characteristic of this tradition of Wisdom teaching, such as we find in the Book of Proverbs and in Egypt.

But in its focus on the Lord's tora ('teaching', 'law'), the psalm seems to reflect a development in which the old stream of wisdom teaching has run together with another current of piety – devotion to tora, the scriptural commandments, teachings and revelations of the Lord. So it may be that Psalm 1 is a relatively late composition, which was given its place at the head of the whole collection of psalms to emphasize a theme dear to the hearts of the final collectors: the theme of God's tora.

1–3   Strikingly, the first word of the Psalter is 'Happiness'. We could translate, 'O the sheer happiness of the person who ... ' With this expression, a way of living is going to be most warmly commended with all the authority of generations of experience. But now come surprises. The first is that the recommendation begins in the negative. There is a road to be avoided; one had best not enter, linger or (worst of all) settle there. This is the way of those hardened in defiance of God and of all that is good. The psalm is not referring to a situation like that in the Gospels, where Jesus reaches out to those, often poor, individuals who have been labelled as 'sinners' by a fastidious and sometimes hypocritical religious elite. The second surprise is that the positive recommendation for 'sheer happiness' amounts to only one thing, and that something few today would have thought of – meditation in the Lord's *tora*. This expression must be distinguished from an absolute, 'the Law', which never occurs in the Psalms. What is meant is the teaching of the Lord in person, imparting his word and his will, his guidance and his grace, and, at the deepest level, his very self. A written form, a scroll, is probably involved, and the content originally would be scripture such as was current at the time of the psalm's origin; eventually, as suggested above, reference might be intended to the Psalter itself. Being a communion with the Lord, such meditation is delightful and fruitful. This thought leads to the great image of a tree planted deep beside running water. Such is the person who by prayer and communion draws from the channels of God's grace.

4–5   The contrasting image for the wicked is the 'chaff', harvest waste. On the hills of Palestine, the evening breeze arises as the earth cools quicker than the sea. As the farmer tossed up his threshed mixture into the breeze, the heavy, good grain fell into a golden heap, while the chaff was whirled away towards the desert. The reference may be to the judgement which is ever close at hand, ever manifesting itself in the trials of life. Or the thought may be of the final judgement, when God makes an end of this world.

6   The teaching of the psalm is summarized with a concluding image – the two ways. One way, that of the just, the Lord 'knows' – he watches over it with love and care; we might say he is beside the traveller in every need, guiding and protecting. The other way, that of the wicked, has no true direction, running out into a trackless waste, lost to all that is good.

The psalm's view of the way that brings happiness and prosperity may seem unrealistic. It is the wicked who often seem to gain wealth, power and success, as other psalms lament. It is possible that with the 'judgement' thought turned to the end of this age, and a new world where the injustices would be put right. But we may rather have the hard-earned insight that, despite appearances, the good way of life in itself finds true happiness and is ever fruitful, while the bad way in itself swerves into misery and a meaningless waste. Here and now the just have the companionship of the Lord on their way, and indeed bear good fruit, often in a mystery. This 'way' means rejecting temptations to corruption and centring all one's thought and delight in 'the Lord's teaching'. A modern application might think of the individual refusing to be carried along by the pervasive influences to greed and baseness that come from every angle; being devoted rather to practices of constant prayer and turning to the word of God; and nourished in the deepest being by the currents of communion that alone give life and joy.

'I Am That I Am, and my counsel is not with the wicked, but in the law of the Lord is my delight, alleluia.' Such was the ancient Christian antiphon, the theme-setting refrain interwoven with this psalm at Easter. In the great poem formed by the year of worship, the figure of the risen Lord was thus put first, as the one who had not made compromise with evil, but was wholly given to the Father's will, and whose cross bore healing leaves and saving fruit for all the world. Under this bright figure, so the church intended, the weak and wayward would gather and come to be made like him, to find all their pleasure in the Lord's word, and all along their way grow in knowledge of him.

Grant, Lord, that through study of your word and nourishment by your grace, we may know the happiness of walking the good way where you are ever at our side.

Psalm 8

Crowned to Love

1 O Lord, our Lord, how glorious is your name in all the earth,
    while your splendour is chanted over the heavens!

2 Out of the mouth of babes at the breast
     you have founded a stronghold,
    to counter your foes,
     and still the enemy and the avenger.

3 When I see your heavens, the works of your fingers,
    the moon and the stars which you have created,

4 what is man that you remember him,
    and the son of man that you care for him?

5 For you have given him little less than the angels,
    and crowned him with glory and honour.

6 You gave him rule over the works of your hands;
    you put everything under his feet,

7 flocks and herds of every kind,
    even the animals of the wild,

8 birds of the heavens and fish of the sea,
    and all that moves along the paths of the seas.

9 O Lord, our Lord,
    how glorious is your name in all the earth!

Although this wonderful psalm can be fairly described as a hymn or song of praise, its form is unusual. It does not contain the usual calls to praise and is throughout addressed to God. The opening line is repeated at the end, and in a choral form (note 'our'), whereas the inner section is markedly borne by a single singer (v.3 'I'). The psalm's theme centres in the sovereignty of the Creator, manifest in royal glory, vanquisher of chaos, maker of the mighty elements, yet, amazingly, willing to make man the earthly agent of his sovereignty, treating him with love and honour. The thought is all enfolded in the wondering adoration of God the only true sovereign and master.

1–2   The address is to 'Yahweh, our Lord / Master *(adon)*'. The chorus utters exclamation at the majestic shining of this 'name' over all the earth, the Name that is the showing forth of God's holy being. It is likely that the psalm is sung at a high moment of such revelation, the moment in the drama of worship when the faithful are conscious of the Creator manifest in victory, and of the world made new. A parallel statement is then made about corresponding worship over or across the heavens; at this climactic moment the heavenly beings also worship and sing responsively of God's glory (Psalm 29.9; Isaiah 6.3). Profound wonder develops in verse 2 that out of the praising mouths of mere 'babes and sucklings' the Lord has founded a fortress against the vengeful chaos, which would return if it could. The context suggests that these 'babes' are the weak and humble worshippers, whose inadequate singing of God's glory is yet used by him to still the avenger. So long as they sing, the chaos is silenced, the meaninglessness repulsed.

3–8   The arresting thought of such humility in God is continued through meditation on the night sky – so brilliant over Jerusalem. The Lord, whose fingers made these bright hosts, yet stoops to attend lovingly to the needs of our tiny race. Moreover, he has given man little less than the angels and has crowned him with royal honour, putting all the other creatures of the earth 'under his feet' – under his dominion. The strong expression 'under his feet' is an echo of the traditional near eastern formulas of kingship, where kings would be commissioned by heaven to rule justly and compassionately, but have conquering power against evil. The kingship which the Lord has bestowed on man is intended as the mediation of God's own rule. There is to be but one kingdom, the just and saving reign of the Creator, and puny man, amazingly, is appointed as the royal steward, the one who is to represent and carry out the wishes of the Lord.

9   The conclusion resumes the opening words. Such use of a refrain here is not just for artistic effect, but brings home the absolutely essential point: through all the earth it is the Lord's name that is glorious; the kingdom, the power and the glory are his and his alone. Woe to man if he should imagine the glory is his own, and come to abuse the creatures entrusted to his care!

The psalm breathes an air of paradise; no mention is made of the failure of man, his treachery and cruelty, the sufferings of the creatures, the obscuring of God's glory throughout the earth. The moment of worship which it seems to reflect was touched with a vision; perfection both primal and ultimate is glimpsed by the eye of faith. The crowned figure appears as representative and head of our race, the ideal that the New Testament declared manifest in Christ (Hebrews 2.6–8; 1 Corinthians 15.20–28; Ephesians 1.22). With the light of the resurrection and new creation, the vision is given again. Amidst all the failure of human responsibility come glimpses of what can and will be. Crowned with honour, close to the angels, the race made new will love those under their rule as they themselves are loved by God.

O God, glorious in heaven and earth, in your grace you make the praises of the humble a stronghold against evil, and have appointed the human race to be your royal minister on earth; grant that we may rule your creatures with love, until with them we are made perfect in joyful subjection to your Son, our Lord Jesus Christ.

Psalm 15

At the Threshold

1   Lord, who will be welcome in your tent,
    who may stay on your holy mountain?
2   One who walks whole,
    and ever does what is just;
    who speaks truth even in his heart,
3   and bears about no slander on his tongue;
    who does his fellow no harm,
    and raises no abuse against his neighbour;
4   who is lowly in his own eyes and humble,
    but honours those who fear the Lord;
    though his pledge prove to his disadvantage,
    he will not go back on his word;
5   he does not lend his money to make ruthless gain,
    and he takes no reward against the innocent.
    Whoever keeps to these words
    shall never be overthrown.

This has the pattern of a question to God relating to his sanctuary, followed by his answer, mediated by priest or prophet. This pattern of teaching is found also in Psalm 24.3–5, and can be compared with inscriptions of other peoples on the gates of places of worship, warning those who would enter of certain requirements of conduct. It is possible that Psalm 15, like Psalm 24, functioned in some processional entry of pilgrims to the holy place. The number of requirements can be counted as ten, like the Ten Commandments (recited on ten fingers?).

1   To the Lord himself the question is put: who may come into the holy place and abide so close to the holy presence? The thought would be focused on the entrance of pilgrims to the great central sanctuary and the 'sojourn' in and about Zion during the festal days.

To come and receive blessing entailed preparation in confession and purification, and earnest thought about what the Lord required of his worshippers.

2   The answer is understood to be given in the name of the Lord. It begins to portray an individual who would be his welcome guest, someone who 'walks whole', living from day to day whole-heartedly for the Lord; not just talking of what is good, but doing it. Sincerity and consistency mark this person, and truth is spoken not just with the lips, but in the heart.

3   This person does nothing hateful or injurious against a neighbour, not spreading slander or shouting abuse either in taunts or rage.

4   Our translation has ancient support and agrees with the Book of Common Prayer: 'he that setteth not by himself, but is lowly in his own eyes'. Others translate: 'in whose eyes a base person is despised', giving a more obvious contrast with the following line. Then the next couplet refers to a promise or sworn oath which the giver in time finds inconvenient or hurtful to himself; one who is pleasing to God will keep it nevertheless.

5   This requirement may seem surprising – literally, 'He does not lend his money on interest'. But such loans are seen in the context of extending help to fellow-citizens fallen into poverty and starvation, a common plight in a country of subsistence farming and uncertain rains. To make a profit out of this misery was prohibited by a sacred law against the charging of interest (Deuteronomy 23.19–20), especially since the practice was sometimes deliberately used to bring about permanent disappropriation and enslavement. Finally, reference is made to the bribing of judges or witnesses to secure condemnation of the innocent, a practice often rife, though condemned by laws and prophets. The concluding sentence draws it all together. A person keeping the foregoing requirements will never be 'moved' or 'thrown down'. In the first place, this promises a safe and secure resting in the Lord's dwelling; and beyond that, his sure support through all the circumstances of life.

The psalm brings home a striking selection of sacred teachings. On the threshold of the holy dwelling, the pilgrim is to ponder especially what the Lord requires in personal relations, for the health of individuals, families, and society. Here are laws of the heart, making for sincerity, humility, reliability, compassion and fairness. It is assumed that the pilgrim comes to a God who has first been known as gracious Saviour, but there is a pattern that this God commands for continuing fellowship, a pattern which must ever be taught afresh, so prone are his worshippers to neglect it. Positive and negative mingle in these requirements, each with its own usefulness. The positive holds up an inspiring ideal, the negative is challengingly specific. In the ancient church the psalm was described as a spiritual harp of ten strings, which we can only play well by the help of Christ. In the music of this 'psaltery' it would seem that the first clause gives the key-note, the ground-tone – the daily life that is 'whole', whole-hearted for the Lord, wholly given to him.

Lord, as ever and again we would cross the threshold to come and rest before your face, grant that we may take to heart your will for us to love our neighbour as ourselves.

Psalm 16

To Know the Path of Life

1   Keep me, O God,
    for I take shelter in you.
2   I say: Lord, you are my Lord;
    I have no good apart from you.
3   As for spirits below, and lords that others delight in,
4   many shall be the troubles of those who turn back after them.
    Their drink-offerings of blood I will not offer,
    nor will I take their names upon my lips.
5   The Lord is my portion and my cup;
    it is you that hold my lot.
6   My share has fallen in pleasant land;
    my heritage shines fair upon me.
7   I will bless the Lord that he counsels me,
    and in the depth of the night instructs my heart.
8   I will set the Lord always before me;
    with him at my right hand, I shall not be overthrown.
9   Therefore my heart shall rejoice, and my glory be glad,
    and my flesh shall abide in safety.
10 For you will not abandon my soul to the land of death;
    you will not hand over your faithful one to see the Abyss.
11 You will cause me to know the path of life,
    fullness of joys before your face,
        and pleasures in your right hand for ever.

This prayer for the Lord's protection is supported by eloquent statements of loyalty and close fellowship with God. This relationship and also the hope of deliverance from death are expressed in such heightened terms, that we may well think the one praying is a king, Yahweh's Elect and Beloved.

1–4 Direct prayer in this psalm is brief and comes at the very outset (v.1). It is followed by an avowal of exclusive loyalty; the psalmist calls Yahweh alone his master (*adon*), and will have no other god.

5–6 The psalmist's close bond with the Lord is now described in striking images. The first resembles something that was said of the priesthood; others had territories as their portion to live off, but the priests, as it were, had the Lord, in that they lived from a share of the offerings. So the psalmist lives only from the grace of the Lord, and only from him receives the cup of salvation. The following images also relate to the sharing out of land. By the casting of lots, borders could be determined and marked with lines or ropes; the psalmist means that his destiny and all that makes up his life is in the power of the Lord to give and shape. And he adds that his share is indeed beautiful – the gift that is the Lord himself.

7–9 The singer is thankful for the Lord's counsel and instruction, and mentions receiving it in the night-watches. Looking always to the Lord, knowing him always close, the singer has confidence that he will not be cast down. In joy and tranquillity his whole being will find peace.

10–11 The expression of trust and confidence, adding force to the opening prayer, now reaches a wonderful climax. God will not abandon to death his covenant-partner, bonded to him in faithful love. A common interpretation is that the reference here is to deliverance from a current danger; he is not to die on this occasion. This would suit the usual trend of Old Testament thought, but it is possible that, beyond this, the passage is coloured by ancient ideas of the continuing life of kings – one made so close by God, called his 'Son', filled with abundant life, would in some way ever remain with God, and this royal destiny would work for the benefit of all his people. The train of thought in our psalm would be that deliverance in a present crisis (v.1) would confirm the king's position in the Lord's choice and favour, and so maintain his hope of everlasting communion. Such an interpretation fits with the fact that in New Testament times the psalm was understood to refer to the new

'David', the royal Messiah, and is applied by the apostles to the risen life of Christ (Acts 2.24f; 13.34f). The conclusion describes fulfilment of joy in God: present knowledge of the Lord as the surpassing good will blossom to perfection on the eternal path in the nearer light of his face.

The psalmist, praying first for God's protection, passes on to affirm his devotion. The Lord alone is his master and God. Recourse to other powers is abhorred. The Lord alone is the very ground of his life, source of sustenance, delight, counsel and instruction. On the Lord he sets his gaze, and trusts that he will not forsake him. In present danger and even, it seems, at the end of earthly life, he trusts that the Lord will bring him through to the path of life, away from the abyss of death, into the fullness of unending joy before God's face. The emphasis of the song is upon total devotion to the Lord. Wanting the Lord alone, the singer gains in and from the Lord all that is good. Having this God only, he has all, and for ever. Following Acts 2 and 13, the Church has seen this psalm as especially prophetic of Christ's resurrection. 'Who is the Path of Life but the Lord himself?' asks Augustine, and proceeds to make relation also to the Ascension and to the believer's destiny through Christ.

Lord Jesus, our portion and our cup, our heritage that shines fair upon us, keep us and counsel us; and by the power of your resurrection cause us to know the path of everlasting life and joy before your face.

The Face and Form of God

1   Hear a just cause, Lord, attend to my cry;
     listen to my prayer from lips without deceit.

2   May judgement for me go out from your presence,
     may your eyes look on what is right.

3   You shall try my heart, when you visit me in the night;
     test me, and you shall find in me no evil purpose.

4   My mouth has not transgressed for rewards of man;
     I have kept to the word of your lips.

5   My steps have held to the way of your commandment;
     my feet have not stumbled from your paths.

6   As I call to you, O God, surely you will answer me;
     turn your ear to me and hear my words.

7   Show the marvels of your faithful love,
     O saviour of those who take refuge
       from rebels against your hand.

8   Keep me as the little one mirrored in your eye;
     hide me in the shadow of your wings,

9   from the wicked that ravage me,
     from my enemies that greedily surround me.

10   They have closed their heart to all feeling;
      they speak in arrogance with their mouth.

11   Now they hem in our steps all around;
      they set their eyes to spread into the land.

12   They are like a lion thirsting for the prey,
      a hunting lion crouching in a covert.

13   Rise up, Lord, confront him, and subdue him,
      by your sword deliver my soul from the evil one.

14   They shall be slain by your hand, Lord, slain;
      their portion shall be to go suddenly from this world.
      But your treasured ones you will replenish,
      and they shall be satisfied with children,
        and have increase to leave to their young.

15   I, found true, will see your face;
awaking, I shall be replenished by the vision of you.

The psalmist prays urgently for deliverance on the grounds that his cause is just, the enemy ruthless and rebellious against God. We may well think of a king who is praying in some national emergency. The enemies seek to plunder and encircle, and have 'set their eyes to spread into the land' (vv.9–11). The prayer takes up the Lord's promises and invitations to his Anointed, and probably is made in connection with vigil and sleep in the sanctuary, in hope of the Lord's drawing near to give his embrace of support and word of blessing and victory.

1–2   With his 'cry' and 'prayer', the supplicant calls for the Lord's favourable attention and decision, in confidence that the cause is 'just' and 'right' and uttered by truthful lips.

3–5   In furtherance of this claim, the psalmist looks to God's testing of his heart. He expects this testing 'in the night', probably referring to the forthcoming night to be spent in the sanctuary; the hoped-for blessing must be preceded by God's trial of his sincerity. And he solemnly affirms that he has kept to the paths of the Lord's requirements.

6–9   In his central petition, the psalmist now asks for the wonders of God's saving acts that spring from his committed love. King and people would shelter in this saviour, away from those who rise up against the divine rule, arrogant and wreaking havoc. For king or for beloved people of God the tender image is appropriate: they would be cherished as 'the little one, daughter of an eye', the tiny figure reflected in the pupil when someone is very close, virtually as a lover who looks into the beloved's eyes, or as the babe at the breast who looks into the eye of the mother. And another remarkable image follows: the psalmist would shelter in God as the fledgling nestles under its mother's wing.

10–12   Further description of the enemies adds to the urgency of the appeal. Pillaging, encircling, they have closed off their organs of reason and feeling, and speak only in self-vaunting arrogance. Having encompassed the borders, they prepare to 'spread into the land'. They keep watch on their prey like a young lion ready to spring from hiding.

13–14   A bold prayer now invokes the Lord to action, to rise up and come with divine sword against the evil one. The translation of v.14 is so uncertain that it is almost best left out of account. Some take it as calling for judgement on the whole brood of the wicked; others as depicting the enemies as made wealthy by God. Our translation finds a contrast – a hope that the aggressors be suddenly swept away, while the Lord's treasured ones be granted well-being and continuance.

15   The psalmist concludes in hope of being granted vision of the face and form of God. In the depth of the night, the Lord, he prays, will draw near and by his revelation fill him with the blessing and strength to go out to the hard task ahead. On awaking after such a visitation, he will indeed be 'satisfied', deeply replenished.

It is remarkable how the most intimate and tender expression of devotion, the most intense and beautiful spiritual moment, is linked here to the harsh affairs of the world. Faced with terrible foes that surround and pillage his land and prepare to overrun it, the psalmist, who is surely the king, is above all concerned to draw near to God; to know such nearness, to see the beauty of God's self-revelation, this is to triumph over the world's wickedness, but not to run away from it. He speaks of a profound 'satisfaction', and would no doubt agree with Augustine's comment here that 'without God, all is emptiness'. And for this satisfaction he looks to the God who comes in the night. In time of fear and loss, God comes through the darkness, and by the beauty of his presence drives away fear and bestows the fullness of his grace.

While the psalm stresses the need for truth of heart in the near approach to God, Christian thought turns to Christ as the pure one through whom disciples too can enter the most holy presence. In the name of Jesus they can shelter under the protecting wings, look into the eye of the beloved, be satisfied with the face and form of God. Into the last night also, the night of death, they can go in sure hope of that encounter and a glorious awakening.

Eternal Father, receive us through the purity of your Son Jesus; and keep us then as the little one mirrored in your eye, hide us under the shadow of your wings, and grant that, through vision of you in all our darkness, we may be satisfied with your everlasting peace.

The Heavens and the Heart

1 The heavens are telling the glory of God,
  and the sky-vault recounts the work of his hands.
2 One day pours out the story to the next,
  one night to another unfolds the knowledge.
3 They use no earthly speech or words;
  their voice cannot be heard.
4 Yet their music goes out through all the earth,
  and their words to the end of the world.
  He has put a tent among them for the sun,
5 which comes out like a bridegroom from his bower,
    and rejoices as a champion to run the track.
6 At one end of the heavens is its rising,
    and its circuit passes over their farthest bound;
  and nothing is hidden from its heat.
7 The Lord's teaching is perfect, reviving the soul;
  the Lord's testimony is trustworthy, making the simple wise.
8 The Lord's precepts are right, and gladden the heart;
  the Lord's command is radiant, giving light to the eyes.
9 The fear of the Lord is pure, and continues for ever;
  the Lord's commandments are true, and altogether just,
10 more desirable than gold, even much fine gold,
  and sweeter than honey, flowing from the comb.
11 Your servant also has light from them;
  in keeping them there is great reward.
12 Who can discern their unwitting errors?
  Cleanse me from my hidden faults.
13 Hold back your servant also from deliberate sins,
    may they not rule over me;
  then I shall be whole, and innocent of great offence.
14 May the words of my mouth find favour,
    and the music of my heart rise before you,
  Lord, my rock and my redeemer.

❦

This has been judged one of the greatest treasures of religious devotion. We imagine a psalmist deeply familiar with ancient hymnody on the lines of verses 1–6, and also familiar with a style of appreciating the Lord's teaching with use of several parallel terms for it ('precepts', 'commandments' etc). Meditating with his harp or lyre in the open court of the temple as night gave way to day, he draws on familiar words from deep within to express his experience of God in the wonders of the heavens and the salvation that comes with his word. Like an emblem of the Lord's revelation in his teaching, the sun has arisen. Near the psalmist, priests are busy with the morning offerings, and he too offers up 'for favour' the music of his meditation (v.14).

1–4a   In profound meditation, the psalmist has become aware of what the ear of itself cannot hear – the singing of the heavens, the sky-vault, and all their lights. They have their being and their orderly and beautiful functions as they in their own way adore their Creator, and hand on within their own kind a testimony to his mighty work, a testimony of praise and thanksgiving passed down from the elements that first witnessed the working of his hands. Down the succession in the species, from day to day, from night to night, the testimony is borne, an inspired singing which bubbles and overflows as, by divine force, the mystery is shown. Their music fills the world, indeed the cosmos, but we do not hear its melody or understand its story. Only an enraptured soul, like that of the psalmist, may become aware that it goes out through all existence, sustaining the gaze of all the elements towards their Creator.

4b–6   The comparisons with a bridegroom and an athlete almost merge. Still today in some Arab lands the newly-wed comes out of the nuptial chamber, where the marriage has been consummated, to great acclaim and a celebratory procession. Our poet sees the rising sun also come forth with joy and ardour, to pass on his way like a champion runner, happy in the strength God has given him. Such an extended, poetical and enthusiastic depiction of the sun is unusual in Hebrew literature. We may contrast the avoidance of the

very word 'sun' in Genesis 1.16, and the terse reference in Psalm
104.19. The passage thus takes on a special significance, preparing
for the sun-like qualities of the Lord's law and teaching – whole and
unblemished, life-reviving, gladdening, constant and enduring,
guardian of justice, illuminating and so making wise.

7–10   In verses 7–9 there are six lines built on the same pattern and
metre, praising the Lord's teaching or law, which is named in six
synonyms. With each synonym the name 'Yahweh' ('Lord') is
emphatically spelt out. We have the impression of the Lord in action,
the Lord making a claim upon his creatures, the Lord giving
authoritative guidance, but all for their good and for their happiness.
His teaching is praised as 'whole, perfect' and 'bringing back the
soul' (restoring and refreshing life); 'trustworthy' and 'making even
the simple wise'; 'straight, plain, true' and 'making the heart glad';
'radiant' and 'brightening the eyes'; 'pure, clear' and 'lasting for ever';
for its 'truth, reliability' and as 'altogether righteous'. The total
picture is of the Lord's word, ruling and teaching with authority, but
faithfully bestowing the blessings of light, life, wisdom and joy. And
verse 10 gathers up the mood of appreciation and love by comparison
with gold and honey: the utterance of the Lord to his world and his
people is utterly precious and desirable, sweet and beautiful. In all
this praise one can feel the effect of the preceding portrayal of the sun.
Here indeed is the sun of the soul, the true light of all existence –
radiant and unblemished, pure and clear, golden and sweet,
enduring, reviving, enlightening, gladdening.

11–14   The meditation has led the psalmist ever closer to the God
who knows and meets every one of his creatures – from the Creator
of the cosmic order, to the Lord who rules and blesses through his
word, and now to the bond with this one worshipper, 'your servant'.
So close to his Lord, he feels his unworthiness. May God cleanse
him from sin which has crept into him unawares, and may he
restrain him from deliberate offences, so easily committed in the
heat of the moment. His longing is to be, by God's grace, 'whole' in
obedience and in love of his Lord. So he has passed from
contemplation of night sky, dawning, rising sun, the light of the
Lord's word, to prayerful encounter with the Lord himself. He has

embodied his meditation in string music and song, and offers it up to find 'favour', acceptance, just as the priests are sending up their morning offerings also 'for favour'. So his music rises, with the song of his lips and the inner melody of the heart. The concluding thought is in the deepest reaches of contemplation: the immediate knowledge of the Lord as 'my rock and my redeemer', the one who saves from perils and from sin, and through his faithful care gives true life in all its goodness.

The marvel of this psalm lies somewhere in its connection of the vast natural phenomena with the individual's moral way. There is perception of a Creator whom the bodies and lights and darks of the heavens revere; what a revelation, what a rapture to know of their melodious outpouring of testimony! There is appreciation of the beneficial and beautiful word of the Lord, that orders and restores the life of his servants. And there is a prayerful communion with him, the individual's rock and redeemer. Through all these runs the thread of contemplation, a thread indeed to guide one with meaning and fulfilment through the vast and complex world. And to the one who gives all, something of beauty in music and poetry, something pleasing to him, is offered up again. The psalmist indeed has found the place of sweet light and gladness.

Christians today still honour their Lord in the psalm with contemplation of him as the Word by whom all was created, and who was further revealed in the Gospel as the Word who saves and directs, cleanses and revives, giving gladness and light. And still the psalm may lead them into the rapture of knowing the cosmic fellowship of praise, where humans are but one kind in the vast array that revere the Creator, and where, like St Francis, they may extend their love to their Brother Sun and their Sister Moon, and even welcome their Sister Death.

Word of the Father, adored by the skies, their lights and their darks, grant us so to embrace your law, that we may be cleansed from all our sins and filled with your light; and so may we ever praise you as our sure rock and faithful redeemer.

Coming Home

1 With the Lord as my shepherd,
   I shall not be in want.
2 In green pastures he will let me lie;
   by still waters he will lead me.
3 He will restore my soul;
   he will guide me in ways of salvation for his name's sake.
4 Even though I walk through the valley of the shadow of death,
      I will fear no evil;
   for you will be with me;
      your rod and your crook will comfort me.
5 You have prepared a table before me,
      a sign to my foes;
   you have anointed my head with oil;
      my cup runs over.
6 Truly, goodness and love will follow me
      all the days of my life,
   and I shall come home to the house of the Lord for ever.

Through the images of the good shepherd (vv.1–4) and bountiful host (vv.5–6) the psalmist testifies to the Lord as his King – caring, providing, mightily protecting. The shepherd was a much-used image for the duties of kingship in the ancient Near East and in Israel, symbolized in sceptre ('rod') and crook. Elsewhere in the Old Testament God is described as shepherd only of the nation, except for one reference to his shepherding of the nation's ancestor (Genesis 48.15). So there is something remarkable here in the extended application of the theme in such a personal way; even in the closing verses we are aware of just the two figures, the Lord and his treasured one, with a background of hostility or danger. If the psalm is the song of a king (David or a successor), all this can be well understood. As representative of his people, and as sharing the royal task with the true King, God, he could dwell on the thought of his relation to this supreme sovereign and shepherd. To him he owes his anointing and the covenant of protection against foes (v.5); from God are sent the angels of covenant-grace to attend him closely on dangerous missions (v.6a); and to God he returns to dwell on the sacred hill of Zion.

1–4 The singer expresses his confidence in the loving care of the Lord. The shepherd's task in the mountainous wilderness of Palestine is one calling for the greatest devotion, skill and courage. Want, hardship, injury and death are never far from the sheep and goats and their young. But the good shepherd knows how to find the pastures of fresh grass where the animals can graze and lie down, and the still pools formed with rocks in the waters of mountain springs, where their thirst, so sharp from the heat, can be safely quenched. So the exhausted life is brought back and strength renewed to follow the wise shepherd on the good ways that he knows how to find. And even in dark ravines, he dispels fear, as he keeps on the watch with his club against foes and his crook to guide and support the little ones.

These images from the shepherd's work are rich in spiritual meaning. Pastures and pools speak of the true life that God both gives and replenishes. The restoring of soul speaks of his delivering from death, and the good ways are properly 'roads of righteousness / salvation', suggesting the joyous route of the rescued one, leading through the 'gates of righteousness' into Zion. The 'valley of the shadow of death' speaks of that land of darkness where death claims dominion, but where the sceptre and crook of the Lord, the signs and instruments of his almighty kingship, are ready to defend and save.

5–6 The Lord is now pictured as host to the psalmist, with only the two figures at the table. The Lord has 'arranged' or 'put in order' the table – spread it with good fare; he has anointed the psalmist's head with oil, a custom for a festive meal; and he has amply filled his cup. The generous gestures of the Lord to this single guest are done in the sight of and over against his adversaries; they are demonstrative, warning foes that the Covenant-Lord will protect this his Chosen One. 'Goodness' and 'Love' are pictured as angelic helpers, representing the generous and faithful love that the Lord has for his Chosen One. These angels are appointed to 'pursue' or attend the psalmist most closely and unceasingly in all his dangerous missions and expeditions. And from these dangers he returns at last to dwell for ever with the Lord.

Many read this psalm with delight in its imagery for divine care and grace, and they readily identify with the psalmist's relationship to the Lord. Especially telling is the assurance of his companionship in the valley of death's shadow, and the confidence of dwelling in his eternal house. But if the psalm is the testimony of the Lord's Anointed, the tender and faithful relationship with the heavenly king is bound up with his royal calling. That calling is for the benefit of all, and so that relationship becomes a fountain of grace and blessing for all. Their life is hidden in his, as he moves in the intimate presence of God. In the Christian context, the psalm has fullest depth when related to Christ and his Father. It evokes the passion and new life of Jesus, and the gifts of the Lord's table. The pilgrims, unworthy, unclean as they are, yet come to know through Christ the true wonders of the pastures of young growth, the still waters, the grace of communion, the angels of love, the comforter in the valley of the shadow of death, and the great home-coming.

O God, our sovereign and shepherd, who brought again your Son Jesus from the valley of death, comfort us with your protecting presence and your angels of goodness and love, that we also may come home and dwell with him in your house for ever.

Psalm 24

At the Everlasting Doors

1   To the Lord belongs the earth and its fullness,
    the world and all its teeming life –
2   For it was he who founded it on the seas,
    and made it firm upon the floods.
3   Who shall ascend the hill of the Lord,
    and who shall stand in his holy place?
4   The clean of hands and the pure in heart,
    who have not lifted up their soul to false things,
        or sworn only to deceive.
5   These shall carry home blessing from the Lord,
    and goodness from God their Saviour.
6   May such be those now seeking him,
    seeking the face of the God of Jacob.   [Pause]
7   Lift up your heads, O gates,
        and be lifted up, you everlasting doors,
    and the King of Glory shall come in.
8   Who is the King of Glory?
    the Lord, strong and mighty, the Lord who is mighty in battle.
9   Lift up your heads, O gates,
        and be lifted up, you everlasting doors,
    and the King of Glory shall come in.
10 But who is the King of Glory?
    The Lord of Hosts, he is the King of Glory.   [Pause]

The psalm evidently accompanied a procession that ascended the sacred hill and entered the gates of the Lord's house. Moreover, it all signified the procession and entry of God himself, and so probably involved the transporting of the ark, symbol of the divine presence and glory. From the opening and closing themes it may be deduced that this grand procession was part of the ceremonies of the chief festival, at the turn of the year in the autumn. With conquering power over the primeval waters, the Creator has secured the living world. The original event has, as it were, been re-lived in the drama of the festival.

1–2 A cry of triumph opens this exciting psalm, as indeed befits the moment of the return of the victorious Lord to his eternal gates (vv.7, 9), the heavenly event mirrored in Zion's festal procession. The living, teeming world belongs to him, and to no other power, because he has conquered chaos, stilled the raging ocean, and built the earth over the subdued waters on the pillars of the great mountains. He enters now as victor, the king who will faithfully sustain the good order of life in all the cosmos. The ceremony was a sacrament in which the work of the Creator was present as at the beginning, and the worshippers rejoiced in the new springs of life.

3–6 As the procession up the sacred way approaches the sanctuary gates, the awe of the holy realm prompts the ancient question: who is fit to endure it? Who may dare to enter as the Lord's guest? The authoritative answer is here put briefly. In action and in motives let the worshipper be 'clean' and 'pure', and let not the soul be lifted up to what is false, or solemn assurances given to deceive. The Lord will not abide the defilement of cruel and treacherous deeds, nor the worship of false gods and the cynical breaking of promises. The worshipper true to these requirements will 'carry' blessing and goodness from the Saviour, returning home laden with such gracious gifts. (For 'Pause' see above, p. 5.)

7–10 An interchange rings out, as the gates are called upon to open, and responding inquiry is made and answered as to who is seeking entry. Like all features of the temple, the sanctuary gates are symbolic of heavenly reality; they are 'gates of eternity', corresponding to the entrance of the victorious Creator's residence above the heavenly ocean. The titles of God are sung out in climactic fashion. As 'King of Glory' he is the supreme power of all the cosmos. As 'Yahweh, Champion in War' he is, further, the Lord who saved and now works through his people. As 'Yahweh of Hosts' he is at the head of the hosts of heaven, or, on another explanation, he is 'Yahweh Omnipotent'. With this final citation of the dread name, the barriers must give way, and the triumphal ascension is accomplished.

One who sings, hears or reads this poem with sympathy is caught up in a most powerful action. An ancient ceremony of worship lives again, and carries us into the very springs of existence. The Creator becomes present, and his work is known in the marvel of its first perfection. The music of triumph celebrates the conquest of evil. And within the cosmic order appears the aspect of revelation and covenant – God's work through chosen ones, and his insistence on the whole-hearted love of truth and goodness. The psalm would gather all so minded, the seekers of God's face, into the throng that passes through the eternal gates.

The church has sung the psalm especially at Ascension-tide, and seen in Christ the manifestation of the King of Glory. Important here is the thought that he alone is worthy to enter, but by his suffering and salvation he makes possible the entry also of sinners who join themselves to him in penitence and faith. And beyond even this rises the faith that, through him, all shall be well, as God saw all was good in the beginning. For to him belongs all the teeming life of the world; he is the good sovereign and shepherd of every creature. He will not forsake them, but in the end will win back every one. The glory of his kingship will be known in his victorious power, justice, and compassionate redemption.

O God, in whose hand is all the plenitude of the earth, restore in us true innocence of life, that, following your Son, we may ascend your holy mountain and rejoice in the completion of your good kingdom.

Psalm 25

The Friendship of the Lord

1 To you, Lord, I lift my soul;
2   my God, I trust in you.
   May I not be put to shame;
       may my enemies not triumph over me.
3 May none who wait for you be ashamed;
   rather let the treacherous be frustrated and put to shame.
4 Lord, make me to know your ways,
   and ever teach me your paths.
5 Cause me to walk in your truth and teach me,
   for you are the God of my salvation;
       all the day long I look for you.
6 Remember, Lord, your tender mercies,
   and your faithful kindnesses which have been from of old.
7 But do not recall the errors of my youth and my sins;
   think of me according to your faithful love,
       for the sake of your goodness, O Lord.
8 The Lord is generous and true;
   therefore he teaches sinners in the way.
9 He will guide the humble in judgement,
   and will teach the lowly his way.
10 All the paths of the Lord are faithful love and truth,
   to those who keep his covenant and his testimonies.
11 For the sake of your name, O Lord,
   forgive my sin that is so great.
12 Who is he that fears the Lord?
   Him will he teach in the way that he should choose.
13 His soul will abide in goodness,
   and his seed will inherit the earth.
14 The friendship of the Lord is for those who fear him,
   and he will make known to them his covenant.
15 My eyes are continually towards the Lord,
   for it is he that shall deliver my feet from the net.

16   *Turn to me and be gracious to me,*
      for I am alone and very troubled.
17   *Relieve the distresses of my heart,*
      and bring me out of my sufferings.
18   *Look upon my affliction and trouble,*
      and put away all my offences.
19   *See my enemies, how many they are;*
      and they hate me with a cruel hatred.
20   *Keep my soul and deliver me;*
      may I not be put to shame,
         for I shelter in you.
21   *May integrity and truth protect me,*
      for my hope, Lord, is in you.
22   *Redeem Israel, O God,*
      from out of all his troubles.

This is an alphabetic composition, each verse beginning with the next letter of the alphabet. The thought in such alphabetic psalms at first sight appears somewhat fragmented, but in the present case we are never far from prayer from affliction. There are three recurring themes: desire for deliverance from suffering, for forgiveness of sin, and for the Lord's instruction and guidance.

1–7   The opening verse strikes the characteristic note of this psalm, the singer being conscious of direct relation to the Lord, lifting his soul in worship and in longing for help in present sufferings. The prominence of treacherous and violent enemies in the psalm perhaps points to the psalmist being a king. He repeatedly asks the Lord to teach him, that he may live daily in the ways of the Lord, knowing well the ways and treading in the path of God's faithfulness ('truth'). Not commandments and principles in themselves are to be treasured, but the One who teaches and guides – 'all the day long I look for you (/ long for you / hope in you'). Recognizing his need of forgiveness, the psalmist appeals to the compassionate aspect of God's abiding love.

8–14 The style here is chiefly that of testimony in praise of God, encouraging to a gathering of worshippers. The message centres on the faithfulness, grace and love of God, which are so wonderfully discovered by those who are humble towards him, willing to be taught, eager for his way. Strikingly, it is said that fear of him finds his friendship; the sense is that those who know him *as God*, the chief factor in every circumstance of their lives, find that he draws close in counsel and companionship (the word rendered 'friendship', *sod*, denotes the circle of trusted intimates who counsel and encourage each other). But significantly, at the centre of this passage the singer repeats his prayer for forgiveness, confessing to great sin; such penitence, he seems to say, is fundamental to the blessedness of intimacy with the Lord.

15–21 The tone of prayer from suffering is here more plaintive and urgent. He asks the Lord to turn his face to him, as he looks in yearning hope ever towards the Lord. In verse 21 'integrity' and 'truth' are best understood as qualities of God that come in the form of angels to protect the trusting one, rather than as human moral qualities.

22 This last verse, outside the alphabetic scheme, makes explicit that suffering and hope of a whole people, which were already borne throughout in the person of the psalmist.

Our psalm has expressed a concentration of yearning hope for God's salvation – that he would deliver from sin and from violent foes. Also, there is openness for his teaching, valued above all for the relationship with him; his ways are the true ways of life; and in a practical consciousness of the divine majesty, the disciple comes to be rewarded with God's 'friendship' – his company and counsel. The element of testimony and the concluding verse especially show how the individual prayer bears in itself a loving hope and intercession for all God's suffering ones.

Father, forgive our sin, which is so great; and cause us to know your ways and to walk in your truth, that we may be saved from cruel enemies, and daily rejoice in the goodness of your friendship.

One thing I ask

1   The Lord is my light and my salvation – whom shall I fear?
     The Lord is the stronghold of my life –
         of whom shall I be afraid?
2   When deadly ones draw near to me to eat up my flesh,
     my adversaries and my foes – see, they shall stumble and fall.
3   Though a host encamp against me, my heart shall not fear;
     though the line of battle rise upon me, yet shall I trust.
4   One thing I have asked of the Lord, and that alone I seek,
     that I may dwell in the house of the Lord
         all the days of my life,
     to look on the beauty of the Lord,
     and seek guidance in his temple.
5   For he will hide me in his shelter in the day of trouble;
     he will conceal me in the covering of his tent,
         and lift me high upon the rock.
6   And then shall my head be high
     above my enemies round about me.
     And in his tent I shall offer sacrifices in joyful thanksgiving;
     I shall sing and make music to the Lord.
7   Lord, hear my voice;
     as I call, be gracious and answer me.
8   My heart recalls your word: Seek my face.
     Your face, Lord, I do seek.
9   Do not hide your face from me,
     or turn away your servant in displeasure.
     You have been my helper;
     do not leave me or forsake me, O God of my salvation.
10   Though my father and mother forsake me,
     the Lord will take me up.
11   Teach me, Lord, your way,
     and lead me on a good path
         against those who lie in wait for me.

12   *Do not give me up to the desire of my adversaries,*
      for false witnesses have risen against me,
          and those who breathe out violence.
13   *But I believe that I shall see*
      the goodness of the Lord in the land of the living.
14   *Wait for the Lord, be strong, and let your heart take courage;*
      yes, wait in hope for the Lord.

A remarkable feature of the prayers of the kings is the combination of harsh military situations with thoughts of tender intimacy in the relationship with the Lord. Our psalm is surely another example. The first section (vv.1–6) prepares the way for the following supplication by making testimony, apparently to a gathering of worshippers, about the confidence that the royal psalmist has in the Lord's salvation. He testifies further of his single-minded desire ever to be close to the Lord and follow his will. And looking forward in faith, he promises to bring thank-offerings in acknowledgement of victory. Then comes the supplication (vv.9–13), into which are woven more reinforcing considerations. The concluding verse may be a choral rejoinder on behalf of the other worshippers, encouraging the psalmist to hope in the Lord.

1–3   The singer begins his avowal of trust and devotion, all in preparation for the supplication that will follow. Throughout verses 1–6 he refers to God in the third person, and seems to address his words to supporting worshippers. With 'my light' we can compare 'thy light' (addressed to Zion) in Isaiah 60.1f; the Saviour comes to his beloved like the rising sun to scatter the perils of night. Enemies are envisaged as a great army. Not in human strength, but by trust in the Lord, the singer would banish fear.

4–6   To the consideration of his trust, the psalmist adds that of his single-minded devotion; his desire is only to dwell in the house of the Lord, and there see the beauty of his revelation and learn his will. And the section concludes with a statement of trust in the Lord's protection in time of affliction. The Lord's 'tent' and 'rock' refer to the Zion sanctuary, where he will keep his beloved safe under his shadow. When the psalmist's head is raised high in victory, he will bring the sacrifices of thanksgiving, singing in psalms the story of salvation.

7–12 After the preparation, the lamenting prayer. The peril seems to have deepened over some time, as though the Lord were 'hiding his face' (v.9), and an apprehension of being forsaken has crept in (vv.9, 12). Verse 8a may be interpreted as a recollection of the Lord's invitations to his worshippers, 'Seek (ye) my face'. Now indeed the psalmist earnestly seeks the face and favourable acceptance of God, and prays they may not be denied him. Verse 19 uses a theme found also in neighbouring countries – the ruler as adopted by God. He pleads for guidance on a 'path of equity', which means also a level path safe from ambush. The reference to 'false witnesses' in verse 12 might refer to false reports about the king to other rulers, or more generally to the pouring out of harmful words and false propaganda against him as war is prepared.

13–14 The supplication is finally reinforced with a statement of confidence that the Lord will not fail him. The 'goodness' of the Lord may have a sense similar to the 'beauty' of verse 4. The thought would be of returning alive from danger to dwell again in Zion. Verse 14 is perhaps best understood as a choral conclusion. The psalmist is bidden to continue in hope of the Lord's help, and so to be brave in the forthcoming conflict.

The pattern of this psalm may give the impression of a person in two minds. Such profession of trust, such apprehension of being abandoned! Is it possible so to believe while doubting, to be both brave and fearful? It seems to have been so for our psalmist. Most urgently he prayed in the face of great dangers, prayed with passion and pathos; but all about his prayer, and in the midst of it, burned beacons of faith, and at the end he is confident of seeing the goodness of the Lord though there remains a waiting. For the waiting will be 'for the Lord', a steadfast looking to him in both hope and trust.

The psalm focuses all that can be desired into one all-sufficient desire: to dwell with the Lord, in that nearness seeing the beauty of his face and receiving his word. This would be in response to the Lord's own invitation to his worshippers, 'Seek my face'. Here is religion in a form not always practised: to seek the beauty of the Lord, the face with which he reveals to a worshipper his particular love and acceptance. And the one who is granted to see this beauty responds with the poetry and music of a song of testimony, the melody of a devoted heart.

Almighty Father, who showed us your face in Jesus, and gave him to be our light and salvation, save us from our adversaries, and set us high upon the rock, that we may dwell in your house, and evermore behold your beauty.

❦ Psalm 29 ❦

The Word in the Thunder

1 *Give to the Lord, you powers above,*
   give to the Lord the glory and strength;
2 *give to the Lord the glory of his name;*
   bow low to the Lord in the beauty of his holiness.
3 *The voice of the Lord against the waters!*
      The God of glory thundered,
   the Lord, against the mighty waters!
4 *The voice of the Lord with might,*
   the voice of the Lord with majesty!
5 *The voice of the Lord breaking cedar-trees —*
   so the Lord broke the cedars of Lebanon.
6 *He made Mount Lebanon skip like a calf,*
   and Sirion like a young wild-ox.
7 *The voice of the Lord cleaving flames of fire!*
8 *The voice of the Lord made the wilderness whirl;*
      the Lord set whirling the wilderness of Kadesh.
9 *The voice of the Lord bowed the oak-trees,*
   and stripped the forests bare.
   Now in his temple all cry, Glory!
10 *The Lord has taken his seat above the ocean of heaven,*
      enthroned as King for ever.
11 *The Lord will give strength to his people;*
   the Lord will bless his people with peace.

The setting of this magnificent hymn seems to be in the ceremonies of the autumn festival at the turning of the agricultural year. Psalm 24 has given us a glimpse of the excitement as the Lord's procession arrived back at the temple gates, after a symbolic re-enactment of the subduing of the primeval waters. Now Psalm 29 takes us on to the climax: the ark returns to the inmost sanctuary, and proclamation is made that the Lord has taken his throne in heaven.

He, and he alone, is supreme over all the cosmos. Our psalm shows the response of worship in heaven and earth, recounts his great work of creative power, and looks to the life that will flow from it.

1–2   The opening call to praise illustrates the universal dimension of worship in the temple, where all heaven and earth meet. The singer directs his call to 'the sons of the gods', the company of the divine attendants and ministers in heaven. They are to ascribe the power and the glory to Yahweh and prostrate themselves before the manifestation of his holiness, his divine majesty. They are picked out in the call to praise to emphasize the significance of the moment – that Yahweh ('the Lord') is revealed as the utterly supreme, the cosmic victor, power above all powers, God above all gods.

3–9b   This central section now glorifies the Lord by giving the grounds for the praise – his mighty deeds preceding this scene of acknowledged triumph. The first and fundamental act was his subduing of the chaos-waters; the ancient poetic style represented this as the cleaving of the chaos-monster (74.12f) or the routing of the waters with a thunder-roar (104.7). Our poet follows this latter tradition: the Lord's thunder-voice went out against the waters, his might and majesty confronted and prevailed over the 'mighty waters' that had pretensions to sovereignty (93.3). The narrative reflects experience of the winter storms in the north of the Davidic kingdom, around the great mountain ranges of the Lebanon and Anti-Lebanon (Sirion, Hermon) From time immemorial in the cultures of Western Asia, the breaking of the long summer drought by the winter rains had been seen as a drama of the gods, a battle that resulted in the earth's new life. For the Israelite faith of our poet, it is the Lord whose power subjugates the cosmic ocean and so gives rain and life. In evoking the first work of creation, our poet passes easily to the portrayal of the annual winter storms, taking them as the Creator's own renewal of his original 'victory'. So we hear of the irresistible power of his voice in the storm that breaks giant trees, shakes the huge mountains, sends flying the dust of the wilderness, and divides the tongues of lightning. This 'wilderness of Kadesh' is probably an area in Syria.

9c-11   The retrospect has given a vivid impression of the Lord's assertion of power in his preparation of life. Now the psalmist returns to the present scene of homage. Verse 9c resumes the opening theme of 'glory': all in God's temple – primarily his heavenly abode with which those in the earthly temple feel united – sing acknowledgement that the glory, the divine supremacy, is his alone. They are responding to the climactic event of verse 10, when the Lord took his throne over the cosmic ocean, pictured especially as the waters gathered above the firmament or sky-vault. His throning above the heavenly ocean signifies that he is the Lord of life; he has subdued and made serviceable the otherwise unruly cosmic waters, and from them he ensures the rains and fountains on which earthly life depends. V.11 is essential to the meaning of the psalm. By his kingship, that rules the great forces to nourish life, the Lord will give vital strength and abundant, healthy growth and provision (*shalom*, 'peace', harmony in nature and society). The word 'strength' resumes the opening call, and with the last words of 'blessing' and *shalom*, the psalm concludes on the good meaning of all the terrible might and majesty that it has evoked.

What terror and consternation, to be out on the mountain-sides in the fury of a winter storm, with the lightning ripping through the skies and the mighty crack of thunder, the tops of great trees splintered off, the forests whirling, the very mountains vibrating, and out to sea a battle seeming to rage between the rearing waves and the missiles from on high! From age-old experience of such awesome tempests the psalm-poetry draws, and makes its tribute to the sevenfold 'thunder-voice of Yahweh'. But this is not a poem on natural phenomena. In the convulsions of nature a meaning is seen and now declared: the Lord – who has a bond with his worshippers and gives them blessings of life and well-being – he, and he alone, is sovereign of the great forces of the cosmos; through all their awesome operations he is at work, preparing his blessings. Even in the shatterings and flames, he is creating life and shaping salvation. In the high moment of worship there has come a glimpse of the eternal moment, the moment which is also the final fulfilment, when all creation acknowledges the royal glory of the Lord and kneels before the revealed beauty of his holiness, rejoicing in his victory, his blessing and his peace.

The Lord's 'thunder-voice' is thus an aspect of his creative Word; within the shattering power is this good Word, the divine purpose and power that makes and shapes the world, the Word known at last, says the New Testament, as grace and truth in the person of Jesus (John 1.1–18). The psalm thus leads to meditation on the power of the Word Incarnate, and on the fullness of glory that is his in the unity of the Father, Son and sevenfold Spirit.

Eternal God, who make and direct all things by your mighty Word, in all the storms of life give us your peace; until we come to sing of your glory, when you bring all things to perfection and appear for ever in the beauty of your holiness.

Psalm 30

Cause for Dancing

1   *I will exalt you, Lord, for you have drawn me up,*
    and not let my foes rejoice over me.

2   *O Lord my God,*
    I cried aloud to you, and you have healed me.

3   *Lord, you have brought my soul up from the darkness;*
    you have restored my life from those gone down to the abyss.

4   *Make music to the Lord, you his faithful,*
    and give thanks to his holy name.

5   *For a moment is spent in his anger, but life in his favour;*
    in the evening tears may visit, but joy comes in the morning.

6   *But when I was at ease I said,*
    I shall never be overthrown.

7   *Lord, in your favour you had made my hill so strong.*
    You hid your face from me, and I was troubled.

8   *To you, Lord, I called out;*
    to the Lord I made my supplication:

9   *What gain is there in my blood, if I go down into the abyss?*
    Can dust thank you? Will it tell of your faithfulness?

10   *Hear, Lord, and be gracious to me;*
   come, Lord, as my strong helper.

11   *You turned my sorrowing into dancing;*
   you took off my sack-cloth, and girded me with joy,

12   *that in glory I should make music to you, and not be silent;*
   O Lord my God, I will give thanks to you for ever.

The psalm in itself appears to be the testifying praise made at the temple by one recovered from grave illness. The situation might thus be like that described in Job 33.24–28 and illustrated by the similar psalm of King Hezekiah after his recovery (Isaiah 38.9–20). But later uses, such as in the re-dedication of the temple, show how the poetry of the psalms resounded with many resonances.

1–3 The singer addresses the Lord in thankful praise, recalling that he answered his cry by healing him, drawing him up, as it were, from Sheol (land of the dead, imagined as a vast pit beneath the subterranean waters). The reference at once to enemies is perhaps a feature from royal psalmody, the king always having to reckon with adversaries that would exploit every weakness and rejoice in his overthrow.

4–5 The setting in a gathering for worship becomes clearer as the singer calls for praising, thankful psalmody from the Lord's 'faithful ones', people of his covenant. The salvation of this one person is cause for joy to all his community. The 'name' here is literally 'remembrance / citation', meaning the name of God as invoked or chanted in praise; gratitude is felt for the very means by which the Saviour makes himself near and available to those in need. In the time of salvation it seems that the suffering was but a moment, or like a night that was dispersed by the coming of glorious day.

6–12 The singer now gives his story. He had grown complacent, and incurred the Lord's displeasure; his world was overturned. He recalls his supplication – how he had put it to the Lord that he would gain nothing from consigning him to Sheol, where all is silence; but if he saved him, what glad testimony he would receive! In such frank and childlike manner the psalmist had pleaded for his Lord to come as his 'helper', or rather 'saviour'. And so, through God's compassion, it had come about. The psalmist was healed, and put away the sack-cloth of penitence; wearing the joyful garb of worship, he comes with dancing step to the altar to offer his song of praise.

Taken as the thankful praise of a person restored from being near death, the psalm well illustrates the practice of telling the story in the community, a testimony to the grace and power of the Lord towards those who, trusting in him alone, cry out to him. The glad worship is filled with poetry, music and dancing; the worshipper's soul is bright with the glory of one who has experienced the Saviour, having confessed and put away the sin of complacency. Not for a day or a season would this worshipper praise God for his healing, but for ever.

And then threads of meaning were found here for the experience of a whole community. In her turn the church has related the psalm to her times of penitence and re-dedication, times when the grace of God has drawn her up from the abyss of death, healed her, clothed her with gladness and led her to a time of dancing, celebrating afresh the resurrection from which her life first sprang. So for the church, as well as for the individual, the psalm prompts the glad testimony of the dance, and the music of love that honours his holy name.

Lord, deliver us in times of ease from the false security that hardens our hearts towards you; and when troubles abound, help us to cry to you with simple faith, and so be granted the morning of healing, and the new life of thankfulness without end.

A Song of Forgiveness

1   *Happy the one whose sin is forgiven,*
    and whose transgression is covered.
2   *Happy the person to whom the Lord imputes no wrong,*
    and in whose spirit is no deceit.
3   *While I would not admit my fault,*
    my bones were consumed through my groaning all day long.
4   *For day and night your hand was heavy upon me;*
    the springs of life within me turned to summer drought.
5   *Then I acknowledged to you my transgression,*
        and no longer covered my wrong-doing.
    I said, I will confess my sin to the Lord,
        and you put away the guilt of my transgression.
6   *Therefore let every faithful soul pray to you*
        while you may be found;
    even when the great waters surge,
        they will not sweep over them.
7   *You are a shelter for me, to guard me from trouble;*
    you will surround me with songs of deliverance.
8   *I will instruct you and guide you in the way you should go;*
    I will counsel you, with my eye watching over you.
9   *Do not be like a horse or mule not yet trained;*
    with bit and bridle their course must be checked,
        or they will not come with you.
10 *Many pains are prepared for a wicked person,*
    but one who trusts in the Lord
        will be circled by faithful love.
11 *Rejoice in the Lord, you faithful, and be glad;*
    sing out, all that are true of heart.

The church included this in its group of 'Penitential Psalms',
appropriately so because of its theme of confession and forgiveness,

although its tone is essentially joyful. In spite of some unusual features, it can best be regarded as thanksgiving and testimony in a gathering for worship. The psalmist tells his story as one who experienced deliverance from trouble, when at last he confessed his sin to the Lord.

1–2 The theme of happiness is introduced strongly. A supremely happy person is envisaged as one whose sin has been 'borne away' or 'covered' – forgiven by God and no longer pretending there was no sin to confess.

3–7 Speaking to the Lord, but for the benefit of the circle of worshippers, the psalmist recounts his own experience. While he was unwilling to confess his sin, he was in physical distress; his bones were troubled, the sap of life dried up within him. But when he acknowledged to the Lord his wrong-doing, the burden of it was lifted from him; the Lord forgave him. The personal story carries a message for every worshipper, committed to God but yet frail and liable to err: through timely prayer they will find the help of God in the midst of peril. When the waters of chaos come rushing like the furious winter-floods down the gullies, the person so reconciled to God need not fear. The psalmist tells the Lord of his trust, and seems to ask with this that the Lord's protection and deliverance may be ever known in days to come.

8–9 This promise of guidance is addressed first to an individual, and is best taken as words of the Lord in response to verse 7. He promises to guide and enable the psalmist to take a good way through the problems of life, ever counselling him and watching over him with loving care. The image of 'horse or mule' adds the thought that on this good way the disciple should walk with the Lord in trust and close accord, not like a horse or mule yet untrained, struggling against bit and bridle, trying to flee its master.

10–11 The conclusion gives first, as a kind of appreciation of the foregoing word of the Lord, a confirming testimony: while the life of wickedness brings its own torments, the life of trust in God is surrounded by his unfailing care. So the final verse summons the circle of worshippers to joyful praise; these 'true of heart' are thought of as those in sincere relation to the Lord, open to him in confession and forgiveness, content to take the way of his guidance, the way of closeness to him.

This much-loved psalm is not stating a dogma that sufferers must be refusing to confess a sin. But it offers advice based on personal experience and finds an echo in many a heart (St Augustine in his last illness had the psalm written on the wall before him). It testifies to a surpassing happiness given by way of confession and forgiveness, and sustained in a walk with the Lord. Here indeed is a positive note for the church's Penitential Psalms; for confession is seen as the gate to a life of happiness, surrounded and upheld by God's faithful love.

But there is another key-word in the psalm – 'trust'; and here is a link to the Christian experience of forgiveness. By trusting in what the Lord has done to overcome the barrier of sin, by trusting in the Lord as the individual's guide and faithful companion, the pilgrim finds that sheer happiness of which the psalmist sings.

Lord Jesus, from whose cross run the springs of life, grant us by faith and sincere confession to be delivered from the drought of a guilt-laden spirit, and so to know the happiness of your guidance and fellowship along our way.

Psalm 36

The Light Shining in the Darkness

1   Sin whispers to the wicked man in the depth of his heart;
    there is no dread of God before his eyes.
2   For he flatters himself in his own eyes
    that his hateful wrongdoing will not be found out.
3   The words of his mouth are harm and deceit;
    he has ceased to act wisely and do good.
4   He devises harm upon his bed;
    he sets himself on a path of wrong and refuses no evil.
5   Lord, your steadfast love is in the heavens;
    your faithfulness reaches to the clouds.
6   Your goodness is like the towering mountains,
        your justice like the great deep;
    mankind and animals alike, Lord, you will save.
7   How precious is your love, O God!
    And under the shadow of your wings
        the children of man take shelter.
8   They shall be satisfied with the good things of your house,
    and you will give them drink from the river of your delights.
9   For with you is the well of life;
    in your light shall we see light.
10 Continue your love to those who know you,
    and your goodness to the true of heart.
11 May the foot of pride not come upon me,
    nor the hand of the wicked drive me away.
12 See how the evildoers shall fall;
    they shall be thrust down, unable to rise.

The psalm opens with a characterization of the evil-doer, a kind of lament to move God to intervene (vv.1–4). There follows the contrasting praise of the Lord's goodness, a trustful statement in support of a prayer (vv.5–9). The supplication at last becomes explicit – a prayer for the Lord's help against the wicked (vv.10–11). Then all is rounded off with an expression of confidence in the downfall of the evil-doers (v.12). The psalmist sings as the representative of the people (vv.9–10), who are carried as it were in his own person (v.11).

1–4   An evil figure is portrayed, one that represents a threat to the psalmist and his people. It is the figure of a ruthless oppressor, having no respect for God, and taking guidance only from the wicked impulse within him. Even in resting he does not desist, but lies thinking out new deeds of evil.

5–9   Addressing the Lord now in direct praise, the psalmist expresses confidence in his good rule of the world. He portrays this rule with a brilliance that should more than counter the preceding image of evil. High as the heavens, firm as the mountain-pillars of the cosmos, inexhaustible as the cosmic ocean is the goodness of the Lord, as known in committed love and a justice that upholds the right and defends the little ones. This God is Saviour of humans and of animals. Under his wings there is shelter for all humankind, for he is wonderfully faithful in his care for his creatures. The thought of salvation here has a focus in the sanctuary of Zion (the 'house', v.8), where the high moments of worship brought the vision of the Creator's presence, radiant with the light of life, and a world made perfect as the garden of Eden (*'edanim*, 'delights'), nourished and made fruitful by the fountain and river flowing from the holy presence.

10–12   To this God, celebrated as Saviour of all the world, the supplication is raised: may his pledged love not cease towards those who do take heed of him and sincerely trust in him. The psalmist, in the royal manner, speaks of himself as the adversary's target: may he not be overcome by the trampling foot or the smiting hand of the aggressor.

While the fluctuation of good and evil prospects, the alternation of hope and fear, is a common experience, the psalm sees the contrast at a deeper level. Through fellowship with God along a way of reverence and truth, the servants of the Lord perceive clearly and with horror the ravages of those who follow only the prompting of evil in their hearts. Against this sad perception, the worshippers cling to a vision born in the holy place, a light from God's presence, a vision of the divine wings that would shelter earth's peoples and animals, and a fountain that gives life to all his creatures. This good vision, with assurance of the Creator's faithful love, is nourished in the faithfulness of worship and persistence of prayer, and it will not surrender to the apparent dominance of the arrogant and cruel heart.

The New Testament has many echoes of our psalm to show both the oppression of sin and the immeasurable grace of God known in Christ, the light and the river of life, the heights and depths of love. In this new context, the psalm still makes its contribution of prayer to sustain the good vision.

O God, the Saviour of all your creatures, shelter your little ones in the covering of your wings, that they may be safe from cruel hearts and hands, and live with joy in the light of your face.

A Passing Breath

1   *I said, I will watch my ways,*
        that I may not sin with my tongue;
    I will keep a guard over my mouth,
        while the wicked are before me.

2   *I kept still and silent;*
    I held my peace, to no avail.
    For my pain increased,

3   *my heart grew hot within me;*
    through my sighs the fire has blazed up,
        and I have spoken with my tongue.

4   *Lord, let me know my end,*
        and what is the measure of my days,
    that I may know how short is my time.

5   *See, you have appointed my days as hand-breadths,*
        and my time is as nothing in your sight,
    for even in the prime of life man is but a fleeting thing.   [Pause]

6   *Each one walks about like a shadow,*
        and they are in turmoil for nothing;
    they heap up, but do not know who will gather.

7   *And now, for what do I wait, O Lord?*
    My hope is only in you.

8   *O deliver me from all my sins;*
    do not make me the scorn of the fool.

9   *I was silent and did not open my mouth,*
    for surely it was your doing.

10   *Take away your plague from me;*
    I am worn out by the force of your hand.

11   *You chasten man with rebukes for wrong-doing,*
        and like a moth you consume his beauty;
    all mankind is but a breath.   [Pause]

12   *Hear my prayer, Lord, and give heed to my cry;*
        do not be silent at my tears.

> *For I am but a visitor with you,*
> *soon passing on, like all my fathers.*
> 13 *Look away from me, that I may have cheer,*
> *before I depart and am no more.*

This seems to be the supplication of someone in grave sickness, a long ordeal which has brought near the reality of death. It is a distinctive and very moving prayer, but all its elements, as usual in lamenting supplications, can be seen as meant to give force to the cry for help; they are considerations to move God.

1–3 This unusual introduction is an indication of the extremity of the suffering. The psalmist had held to the ideal of suffering patiently, acknowledging the hand of the Lord, and being careful not to seem to question the justice of God in the hearing of the ungodly. But his condition grew only worse, and the inward fires, as though fanned by his sighs, have blazed up and caused him now to cry out to God.

4–11 The resultant prayer is still controlled by humility. It begins without reproaches; the sufferer simply asks that he may be helped to accept the brevity of his life, as of all human life. The thought is developed as a consideration to move God – so short is human life, even at its best, so insubstantial, with any wealth and achievements quickly snatched away; then (it is implied) may not the little time that this sufferer has be more happy, especially as all his hope is in the Lord alone? Again in humility, he does not claim to be blameless, but asks to be saved from his sins (from their consequences), recognizing that God chastens man 'with rebukes for wrong-doing', eating away his vigour and health as a moth consumes a garment. With this readiness to accept God's justice, the sufferer pleads also that time of silent acceptance, and prays for God to take away his 'stroke' or 'blow' of sickness.

12–13 The concluding prayer is that God, for his part, should not stay silent, but speak the word of comfort and salvation. The brevity of life is urged again. As 'sojourners' without rights of possession, so human beings are granted a little stay on God's land, before passing on to their abiding home in the abyss of silence, Sheol; but sojourners and guests, because of their weak position, were specially protected and honoured, and so the comparison makes an appeal to the Lord's faithful kindness. The concluding verse is full of pathos – that a little cheer might return if God but looked away from the sufferer. But again, there is the note of humility; it is the judging eye of God which should look away, for the psalmist does not claim the merit to satisfy its searching purity.

This touching prayer reflects the dominant religious outlook of most of the Old Testament, an outlook which did not expect real life for the individual beyond death. Even the hope of a kind of continuance through children is not mentioned here. In due course, the hope of God's good purpose for the future of his creatures was to develop in several ways, but in the meantime, for many centuries, the old austere outlook encouraged a keen appreciation of the light of life while it was given, and of the reality and glory of God. Eternity was his alone, and humans were a quickly-passing phenomenon best occupied (so our psalm teaches) in looking to him with humility, patience and hope, and certainly not in heaping up wealth and self-importance. The theme is taken up in the New Testament in the new context of the resurrection: this fleeting life is a pilgrimage to the true home in God's eternal bliss (Hebrews 11.13–16; 1 Peter 2.11).

Eternal Father, see the tears of those who suffer, and in your compassion deliver them; give us wisdom at all times to know that we are pilgrims passing soon through earthly life, and may all our hope be in you.

The Hind that Gasps for Water

1   As a hind pants for rills of water,
    so pants my soul for you, O God.

2   My soul thirsts for God, for the living God;
    when shall I come and see the face of God?

3   My tears have been my bread by day and night,
    while all day long they say to me, Where is now your God?

4   Yet I remember, as I pour out my soul before me,
    how I passed through the crowd,
        and led the procession to the house of God,
    in a tumult of praise and thanksgiving,
    as the pilgrim throng rejoiced.

5   How you are bowed down, my soul,
        and how you moan before me!
    Wait still for God, for I will yet give him thanks,
        my saviour and my God.

6   My soul is indeed bowed down before me;
    for I remember you, Lord, from Jordan's source,
        from Hermon's slopes and Mount Mizar.

7   Deep calls here to deep with the roar of your water-spouts,
    and all your breakers and billows sweep over me.

8   O that the Lord would command his faithful love
        in the day-time,
    and that his song would be with me in the night,
        praise to the living God!

9   But I say to God my rock, Why have you forgotten me?
    Why must I go about mournfully,
        while the enemy oppresses me?

10 As though to crush my very bones,
        my adversaries speak cruelly against me,
    as they say to me all the day long, Where is now your God?

11 How you are bowed down, my soul,
        and how you moan before me!

Wait still for God, for I will yet give him thanks,
my saviour and my God.

        ⚜

1   *Give judgement for me, O God, and take up my cause*
       against an unfaithful people;
    deliver me from the deceitful and wicked man.
2   *For you are God my refuge; why have you rejected me?*
    Why must I go about mournfully,
       while the enemy oppresses me?
3   *O send out your light and your truth, that they may lead me,*
    and bring me to your holy hill and to your dwelling,
4   *that I may come to the altar of God,*
       to God my joy and gladness;
    and with the lyre I will praise you, O God, my God.
5   *How you are bowed down, my soul,*
       and how you moan before me!
    Wait still for God, for I will yet give him thanks,
       my saviour and my God.

        ⚜

These psalms were often joined as one. The two together in fact form one supplication of great beauty. The first part is chiefly a lament portraying and holding up to God the dire situation, while the second part brings the climax of direct petition. The refrain, concluding each of three equal sections, takes the form of the singer's exhortation to his own soul, which he pictures as a penitential mourner before him. He is 'remembering' (invoking) God 'from the land of (River) Jordan' and 'the Hermons'. But since he is there overwhelmed by breakers amid the roar of the two 'deeps', it seems that this geographical reference is picture language for a situation near to death, such as is often imagined as the watery mouth of the abyss. That the singer is not a private sufferer appears from his having a dispute with a *goy* ('nation / people') that has broken covenant (43.1). Psalms 44 and 45 are definitely psalms of the king and nation, and if the singer of our psalms is the royal figure, we can well understand his leading of the festal procession (42.4) as the festal role of the king. In a time of suffering, king and people are here plunged into mourning and penitential rites, remote indeed from the joyous scenes of festal celebration.

42.1–3 The soul's longing for God is here a matter of concrete circumstances – political and social calamity. The singer brings it before God with a striking image: in a drought-stricken land, a hind or doe (perhaps with young) is wandering desperately, straining upward to catch the scent of water. The words 'living God' suggest the phrase for 'living water', fresh water from a spring (compare Jeremiah 2.13). To 'see the face of God' meant to meet him in his sanctuary, especially in the high moment of his gracious appearing in the festivals. Verse 3 indicates a time of penitential fasting; also to move God comes the report of mockery regarding his care, the mockery of foreign peoples. The nation's mourning is a challenge to God's name.

4–5 The lament continues by drawing the contrast between the present state of mourning and past scenes of festal worship. The psalmist himself seems to have led the procession with dancing step up the sacred hill and into the house of God. Such processions were a climax of the drama of worship, not just ceremony for ceremony's sake. God's victory and new creation, his self-manifestation in light and life – such were the meanings of the solemn entry, and the pilgrim throngs danced also and shouted thunderous acclaim to their God and Saviour. But how different now! In dialogue with his soul, the singer exclaims 'How you are bowed down' – how deeply you mourn, with gestures of crouching, rolling in the dust and moaning! But hold on in faith, he continues, and the time of thanksgiving will surely come again.

6–8 Now in direct address to God, the singer tells of his mourning soul, and how he is 'remembering' God – calling upon his name – from the mouth of the abyss; the waves and billows of the death-land sweep over him. The poetry of his appeal is heightened as that dreadful situation is pictured in terms of the place where the Jordan begins. Down the slopes of the mighty massif of Hermon cascade the results of winter's rains and snows, and the turbulent waters roar together. 'Mount Mizar' ('Mount Littleness') is unknown – presumably one of Hermon's heights. The awesome scene gives a powerful image of the dire situation that is now lamented.

9–10   The lament is resumed with full force: God in bond with the sufferer, and yet forgetting him, leaving him to the mockery of the enemy! The refrain ends the lament with a note of trust, which carries its own appeal, as the soul is exhorted to wait for this one claimed as its champion.

43.1–5   The singer prays for deliverance from an 'unfaithful nation' that has not kept covenanted loyalty with him; the 'deceitful and wicked man' may be their leader. God's 'rejecting' is in stark contrast with the various phrases throughout the composition for the very close bond that had existed. The 'light' and 'truth', like the 'faithful love' of 42.8, are to be sent on a mission of salvation from God's presence, angels that personify his fidelity and his will to save. They are imagined as leading the rescued sufferer to testify of his deliverance in the temple.

This is the supplication of one oppressed by great suffering, yet in recollection and in hope glimpsing the light of salvation, and gathering all the resources of soul and faith to call it into the present darkness. One picture of distress succeeds another to move the divine compassion: the thirsting hind that cries to heaven; the overwhelming waters of the Abyss; the bowing and moaning of the mourning soul. Can it be that 'my God', 'the God of my life', 'my rock', 'the salvation of my face', should now forsake and reject? Where now all that joy in worship, that light of his face, that grace for one that led others in his praise? Wait, wait, hold on to your trust – so the sufferer's own heart speaks; the saviour will again appear in all his light of faithful love.

The lament is echoed in the words of Jesus when in the shadow of death (Mark 14.34; John 12.27). His way to the altar of sacrifice was in the end to be shown as the supreme way of light and truth and gladness. So down the centuries his followers have approached the eucharist with the prayer for the Lord's light and truth to lead them to the holy mountain and the music of joy and thanksgiving, to lead them up the way from the waters of death to the beauty of God's face.

God of our life, our rock and our salvation, when we feel forsaken and rejected and our soul is bowed down, send out your light and your truth to lead us to your holy dwelling, where we may see the beauty of your face, and at your altar give thanks for your salvation.

Psalm 45

The Lord's Anointed and the King's Daughter

1 My heart is astir with a gracious word;
   I speak my poem for the king,
      my tongue like the pen of a rapid writer.

2 You are fair above the children of man;
   grace is poured on your lips,
      for God has blessed you for ever.

3 Gird your sword on your thigh, O mighty one;
   gird on your majesty and glory.

4 And in your majesty ride on victorious,
   because of truth, humility and justice.

5 Your right hand shall teach you dread deeds
      with your sharpened arrows;
   peoples shall fall under you, amidst all foes of the king.

6 Your throne is of God, for ever and ever;
   the sceptre of your kingdom is the sceptre of justice.

7 As you have loved right and hated wrong,
   God, your God, has anointed you
      with the oil of gladness above your fellows.

8 Myrrh, aloes and cassia are on all your garments;
   from halls inlaid with ivory,
      stringed instruments delight you.

9 Kings' daughters are among your noble women;
   at your right hand stands the queen in gold of Ophir.

10 Hear, O daughter, consider and incline your ear,
   and forget your own people and your father's house.

11 And the king shall delight in your beauty;
   since he is your lord, give honour to him.

12 Then the fair city of Tyre shall make gifts;
   the richest of peoples will seek your favour.

13 The king's daughter is all glorious within;
   her clothing is enwrought with gold.

14 *She shall be led to the king in raiment of needlework;*
    her companions, the maidens that follow her,
        shall also be led to you.
15 *With joy and gladness shall they be led,*
    and shall enter the palace of the king.
16 *In place of your fathers shall be your sons;*
    you will make them princes throughout the earth.
17 *I will make your name remembered through all generations;*
    so the peoples shall praise you for ever and ever.

This 'poem for the king' (v.1) comes from the heart of the royal wedding ceremony. The singer tells of his inspiration (v.1), addresses praise and blessing to the Lord's Anointed (vv.2–9), speaks counsel and blessing to the bride (vv.10–12), depicts the bride in her beauty and her entrance into the king's palace (vv.13–15), and concludes with promise to the king of enduring life through children and name (vv.16–17). The psalm is best taken as preserved from the ceremonies of the Davidic dynasty.

1 The singer's introduction describes his inspiration and indicates that it is a poem for the king which he is now to utter. So he tells how his inspired heart seethes, driving up to his tongue 'a good word', a gracious message from God. His tongue will dart swiftly and surely like the pen of an expert scribe.

2–5 Directly addressing the king, the psalmist declares and confirms the divine blessing which gives him beauty beyond that of mankind and inspired grace of speech; and it is a blessing 'for ever'. In this eternity is the thought of an enduring dynasty, but probably also of the king's personal bond with God. Still bestowing blessing, the singer uses the imperative: 'Gird ... succeed ... ride.' So God will enable his Chosen One to ride forth in majesty and conquer for the cause of (or 'because of') faithfulness, humility and right. The strong language of conquest bestows divine power to succeed against evil on behalf of God's kingdom.

6–7   The throne of the Lord's Anointed can be called the very throne of God and so eternal – his reign serves and expresses God's reign (1 Chronicles 29.23; 28.5; Psalm 110.1). Likewise his sceptre, symbol of the rule, is the very sceptre of God, the sceptre of eternal justice. The Anointed One who is true to this justice, devoted to right, opposed to corruption, he is truly raised by God's anointing above all his companions (including other kings).

8–9   Thought now turns towards the union of king and bride. The oil of the anointing, from the very hand of God (v.7), contained precious aromatic spices and flowed down from the head to the garments. The myrrh, aloes and cassia on the garments are now seen as preparation for the royal love. From rooms adorned with ivory inlay, the music of plucked strings sounds out to delight the king, being perhaps commenced now for a procession, and hence the reference to the king's 'precious ones' or 'jewels', noble and royal women. At the king's right hand, the bride takes her position as queen and consort, adorned (perhaps crowned) with gold from Ophir (thought to be in Arabia or Somalia).

10–12   The singer now addresses her. She is beginning a new life, and he bids her apply herself to her new role and not be distracted by recollection of what had been familiar in her life hitherto. She is to give her devotion to her royal husband, her 'lord'. But if much is asked, much will be given. The maritime city of Tyre may be mentioned as an example of great neighbours; even such peoples, wealthy from world trade, will come to honour her with gifts and seek her favour.

13–15   The singer describes what is probably a development in the ceremony. The bride has gone 'within' and is now clothed in beautiful raiment, enwrought with gold and embroidered. Followed by her train of virgin-companions, royal maids of honour, she is led into the king's residence.

16–17   In conclusion the singer returns to direct address to the king, a kind of blessing: by God-given destiny he will have children for the extension and continuance of his reign. The 'name' in verse

18 is not given, for what is meant is the dynastic life; there will always be a 'David' to serve and express God's kingdom.

While details of the wedding ceremony remain uncertain, the main lines of thought are clear and striking. The prophet-poet, conscious of a mighty inspiration, delineates a royal figure chosen and empowered by God to effect his reign; to this Anointed One is promised power to conquer, by way of and for the sake of justice, humility and faithfulness. The extension and everlasting continuance of this royal ministry is the aspect which then comes to the fore. A 'daughter' from another kingdom offers herself in humility and love, and from the union will come the blessing of continuance.

In the course of time, long after the overthrow of the Davidic kings, Jewish interpreters related the psalm to the Messiah and his people. In the New Testament such an interpretation is assumed to be shared, and verses 6–7 are used to show Christ's superiority to angels (Hebrews 1.8). The psalm became a fountain of poetic meanings. For Christians the 'good word' of verse 1 was the Word (John 1.1) and the 'king's daughter all glorious within' could be expounded as the true church, simple and loyal, as against outward show of wealth. Most enduring are applications which stem from the psalm's own theology. Where this fidelity has been maintained, the warm poetry has led the soul of individual or community towards the everlasting throne of God by way of love for Christ. Adoring him, and forsaking all other, the soul finds in him all the meaning of God's eternal kingdom.

Eternal Father, lead us into the love of the Lord Jesus, that our hearts being ever stirred by this love, we may live in the cause of faithfulness, humility and justice.

Psalm 46

God With Us

1 God is our refuge and stronghold;
  our help in troubles, and very ready to be found.
2 Therefore we shall not fear though earth sways,
  and mountains reel in the depth of the sea;
3 though its waters roar and foam,
  and the mountains quake at its rearing pride.   [Pause]
4 But there is a river
    that gladdens with its streams the city of God,
  the holy dwelling of God Most High.
5 Since God is in her midst, she shall not be shaken;
  God helps her as morning breaks.
6 When the nations rage and kingdoms reel,
  he utters his voice, and earth melts in consternation.
7 The Lord of Hosts is with us;
  the God of Jacob is our stronghold.   [Pause]
8 Come, see the acts of the Lord,
  the destructions he makes on earth.
9 He makes an end of wars to the bounds of the earth;
  he breaks the bow and snaps the spear,
    and the shields he burns in the fire.
10 Be still and know that I am God;
  I will be exalted over the nations,
    I will be exalted over the earth.
11 The Lord of Hosts is with us;
  the God of Jacob is our stronghold.   [Pause]

This is one of the splendid psalms that reflect the sacramental drama of the autumn festival. Some of these centre on a symbolic deliverance of the city where God dwells, and among them is the present psalm. With statements of praise and thankful confidence it combines exposition of what the drama signifies: the chaotic forces represented by the primeval ocean and by rebellious nations have been subjugated, life and peace have been secured from the holy city to the ends of the earth. While this great sacrament bore in the first place on the need for rains, growth and social revival at the beginning of the autumnal new year, it opened such visions of a perfected world that the worshippers were caught up in an experience of God's ultimate purpose.

1–3 The opening is a kind of exclamation in response to the coming or manifestation of God as Saviour. He is praised as a stronghold amidst perils and as answering the prayer of distress – he 'lets himself be found', hearing and intervening. Underlying the thought of verses 2–3 is the idea that the Creator mastered and made serviceable the primeval waters, and fixed the earth over them on mountain-pillars; when the world's good order is threatened, the waters rage as of old and the mountains and earth rock, until the Creator renews his first work. This work of renewal was the theme at the heart of the festival.

4–7 The 'city of God', the place of the temple and the festival, is seen in such psalms in transfigured glory. It is the earthly counterpart of God's heavenly throne, and is seen as the Eden-like place from which the river of life flows out to give life to the world. The humble fountain of Gihon and its channels that run under the city and along the Kidron valley are a glimpse of this poetic ideal. This 'river' now is a sign of the cosmic waters made serviceable, and so of the life with which God will 'gladden' city, people and world. The dramatic ceremonies, reflected and expounded in verses 5–6, represented a time of peril, a war against the holy city; and then, with the break of morning, the manifestation of God's presence, his salvation of his city, his word that routs the chaotic powers. The refrain (v.7) is a victory chant, ascribing the glory to the Lord alone.

8–11 The worshippers are summoned to see for themselves the results of the Lord's victory, probably symbolized in some way (we can compare 48.8 and the many symbolic representations done by the prophets). A vision arises of weapons in piles across the earth, broken up and burned – a beautiful destruction, for the Lord has ended wars, as only he could. And his voice sounds out to all peoples: he bids them to 'desist' from their schemes and their rebellious and divisive ambitions, and to recognize where true power lies. Then the choral song of victory and thanksgiving rounds off the psalm.

With economy and powerful imagery, the psalm has testified of the Lord who is ready to be found, to answer and make himself known in times of trouble. When it seems that the world is falling apart and evil breaking loose, he is a refuge and stronghold. The night of fear is banished by his rising sun; his presence is known in the midst of the troubled ones. He sends his life giving streams into the desert places. Such is the testimony from ceremonies that distilled the experience of many generations, people who suffered much and lived precariously, and yet witnessed to the divine faithfulness. The ceremonies also projected an ideal. Entering through worship the timeless moment when God is manifestly supreme, the pilgrims see war destroyed and a world made glad for ever.

Their 'God with us' was to be the church's theme. In Christ, our Immanuel ('God-with-us'), the morning had broken, and the river of life flowed to the thirsty. Through him, God let himself be found, the stronghold of salvation. Not yet the completion on earth, not yet the end of hatred and killing; but with new force the psalm's vision of peace shines out, inspiring and sustaining until the day of fulfilment.

O God, our refuge and strength, grant we may not fear though troubles rage around us; send into our hearts your river of peace, and rise upon our darkness; so may we know that you are with us always.

❦ Psalm 48 ❦

The Parable of Faithful Love

1　Great is the Lord and most glorious
　in the city of our God.
2　His holy mountain is the fairest of heights,
　　the joy of all the world;
　Mount Zion is the mountain of heaven,
　　the city of the Great King.
3　God is her citadel;
　he has shown himself to be a tower of refuge,
4　For see, the kings assembled;
　together they swept on.
5　The instant they saw, they were dumbfounded;
　they were filled with terror and dismay.
6　Quaking seized them then and there,
　writhing, as of a woman in labour.
7　With a mighty wind from the desert,
　you broke up the galleons of war.
8　We have both heard and seen in the city of the Lord of Hosts,
　　in the city of our God:
　God has established her for ever.　　[Pause]
9　We have enacted your faithful love,
　in the midst of your temple, O God.
10　As your name, O God, so also your praise
　　reaches to the ends of the earth;
　your right hand is full of justice.
11　Let Mount Zion rejoice and the daughters of Judah be glad,
　because of all your judgements.
12　Walk around Zion and encompass her,
　and count up her strong towers.
13　Mark well her rampart, and study her citadels,
　that you may tell the next generation:
14　This is our God, our God for ever and ever;
　it is he that shall lead us out from death.

Like the two preceding psalms, this psalm of praise is best
understood in connection with the ceremonies of the autumn
festival. It responds to a symbolic act of salvation, and at the same
time conveys its meaning. It is the salvation of Zion which has been
'enacted' or 'represented' (v.9), and the praise of God for this
assurance is joined with praising appreciation of his holy place. This
is another striking example of the adaptation of more ancient poetic
and religious tradition; several threads can be traced back to older
Syrian culture, but all is re-created as a resounding tribute to
Yahweh, Lord of Hosts, and his temple in Jerusalem. The structure
of the psalm reflects throughout the festal ceremony.

1–2 Praise of the Lord who is present in glory continues into
praise of his city and temple hill; this continuation is a fitting
introduction to what the psalm is about to unfold – God's work of
salvation in and through his sanctuary-city. An ancient and
widespread conception is here applied to Zion: she is given a rich
role and meaning – centre of blessing for the world, a mystery where
the heavenly throne of the King of all creation is known on earth. In
the light of such a faith, the humble hill of Zion is seen indeed as
'the fairest of heights', and she can be called 'mountain of heaven'.

3–7 The singer now recounts an act of deliverance, and the
indications are that this was not a historical event but a symbolic or
sacramental action. Just as the prophets Jeremiah and Ezekiel were
later to enact the *destruction* of Jerusalem, so the festal ceremony
could enact *salvation* for this 'city of God'. The singer's task is to fill
out the meaning of the symbolic action with his poetic word and
song. He begins with the essence: God has himself been her citadel
or stronghold; he has made himself known as her impregnable
tower. Now comes the detail: the worshippers are prompted to
imagine how the world's kings consorted together and joined forces
to sweep on like a flood against Jerusalem. But coming into view of
that glorious citadel and tower, the glorious presence of God, on the
instant they were struck down with awe and trembling. With his
east wind God broke the mighty fleet of the attackers. The poetry

here will have passed down from ancient use in the Lebanon, where devastating winds from the eastern desert sometimes blow across the lofty mountain ranges and pour down onto ships near the coast. In the symbolic ritual, even at landlocked Jerusalem, the picture was eloquent of shattered human arrogance.

8–10 In choral style there comes a response of summary and affirmation: the worshippers have both heard and seen the sacrament of deliverance and know its meaning, namely that God has secured his city for ever. In verse 9 the first verb (basically 'to make a likeness') is taken abstractly by some translators, 'We have imagined / reflected on'; but the direct concrete meaning fits the context well: 'We have represented / mimed.' The acted parable, the sacred drama (done in the centre of the temple, perhaps the main court) has shown forth God's faithful love in defending his city. For this, his love, even more than for his power, God's name and glory shine from Zion to the ends of the earth. His right hand, representing his deeds, is seen to hold the sceptre of righteousness.

11–14 The concluding call to praise summons both the holy hill and also the 'daughters of Judah' – either the young women who would take the lead in victory celebrations with tambourines, chants and dances, or perhaps the daughter-towns of Judah. Finally the worshippers are invited to make procession around the city, noting her defences and so being inspired to hand on the testimony to this Saviour God.

Our psalm has brought forward one of the richest biblical images – the holy city of God, that sanctuary where heaven is disclosed, and the presence and powers of the sovereign Creator are encountered. As an embodiment of the meaning of worship, this 'city' and 'fairest of heights' ever stands for humble pilgrims to come and see, hear and know. But the wonder of such psalms is that originally all this meaning was woven as one with the need for daily bread, for the defence of the realm, and for social justice. How great the tension for faith, then, when Zion was destroyed! Some looked for a future vindication, while some found Zion to be an image only for the church, the eternal home in God's presence.

This latter interpretation has been immensely meaningful to Christians down the ages, but all the better when the relation to the worlds of nature, politics and community is strongly maintained. In this spirit the sacrament of God's love can still be celebrated with joy, and so there can be given the assurance of his defeat of the assaults of evil, and his leading of his world (as the Upanishad has it) from delusion to truth, from darkness to light, from death to life.

Lord, in our hymns and preaching, our prayers and sacraments we make a likeness of your conquering love, and believe you are at work in all this our worship; grant us so to stand in your fair and holy city that we may be able to carry forth your redeeming power and kindle the faith of generations to come.

∽ Psalm 51 ∽

My Sacrifice

1   *Be gracious to me, God, in your faithful love;*
     in the abundance of your compassion blot out my offences.

2   *Wash me thoroughly from my wickedness,*
     and cleanse me from my sin.

3   *For well I know my offences,*
     and my sin is ever before me.

4   *Against you only have I sinned,*
     and done what is evil in your eyes,
     so you will be justified when you speak,
     and in the right when you give sentence.

5   *Truly I was born in wickedness,*
     a sinner when my mother conceived me.

6   *Yet you desire truth in the inward parts,*
     and in the heart's depths you will teach me wisdom.

7   *Cleanse me with hyssop and I shall be clean;*
     wash me and I shall be whiter than snow.

8   *Cause me to hear joy and gladness,*
     that the bones you have broken may rejoice.

9   *Hide your face from my sins,*
     and blot out all my misdeeds.

10   *Create for me a pure heart, O God,*
     and renew a steadfast spirit within me.

11   *Do not cast me out of your presence,*
     or take your holy Spirit from me.

12   *Bring back to me the joy of your salvation,*
     and uphold me with your gracious Spirit,

13   *that I may teach the rebellious your ways,*
     and sinners to return to you.

14   *Deliver me from guilt, O God, the God of my salvation,*
     and my tongue shall sing of your goodness.

15   *Lord, open my lips,*
     and my mouth shall proclaim your praise.

16   *For you have not required a sacrifice;*
     if I gave a burnt offering, you would not accept it.
17   *My sacrifice, O God, is a broken spirit;*
     a heart that is broken and crushed, O God,
        you will not despise.
18   *Do good to Zion in your favour;*
     build up the walls of Jerusalem.
19   *Then you will accept the offerings of fellowship,*
        sacrifice burnt and whole;
     then indeed shall they offer up bulls on your altar.

The ancient heading of this psalm has an additional note proposing
that the occasion was 'when Nathan the prophet came to him
(David) when he had come to Bathsheba'. Such notes, however,
generally seem to be deductions from words in the psalm. This
psalm as a whole (including vv.18–19) may rather speak for a king
in his representative capacity. Speaking in individual terms, he
would be leading the penitence of the people incorporated in him,
and so naturally concludes with the prayer for the well-being of
Zion. The use of the psalm in later Jewish worship on the Day of
Atonement and in the church on Ash Wednesday shows how it can
speak for the community. It has indeed been used in the church
more than any other psalm, having been included in each of the
seven Hours of the daily Office.

1–4   The first word in the Hebrew is the plea for grace; on
nothing else can the prayer be founded but the gracious compassion
of God. May he then be gracious according to his pledged and
faithful love and the abundance of his tender pity, and so act to put
away the supplicant's rebellion and wrongdoing. May he expunge
them as from a heavenly record, and wash clean the sinner as clothes
were pounded in water. The rebellious offences had been deliberate,
and the penitent one confesses to well knowing them and having
them ever before him. So clearly does he see that his wrong-doing
was an affront to God, a rebellion, a breach with him, that he says
'Against you, you only, have I sinned' – surely not denying harm to

others, but expressing the overwhelming sense, the terrible insight, that the wrong-doing was first and foremost against the Lord.

5–8 A literal rendering would give: 'Behold, in iniquity I was travailed with, and in sin did my mother conceive me,' but the thought is of his own radical waywardness, a sense of being so profoundly unworthy of God that he yearns to be purified and created anew, so that faithfulness and spiritual wisdom may possess his deepest being. Such profound purification is the divine act signified in a rite of sprinkling water from a sprig of the hyssop shrub. Under the symbol, God's work, and that alone, can make the sinner 'whiter than snow' (similarly Isaiah 1.18). Then will come the time of joyous festival, when the people, no longer like 'broken bones', in wholeness sing and dance their songs of thanksgiving.

9–13 Prayer is renewed that God will put away and expunge the sins, create for the penitent a pure heart, and renew a firm spirit within – renew the inner life with all the firmness and strength to keep God's way. In verse 13 it may be especially the ideal of the Lord's Anointed which is in mind – serving in the near presence of God, empowered by the holy Spirit.

14–19 This begins literally 'Deliver me from blood / bloodshed', and is perhaps best understood to refer to guilt deserving death. Relieved of such guilt, the psalmist will sing of God's 'rightness', which clearly denotes his grace and mercy. 'Open my lips' implies the act of salvation, which fills the mouth with the song and power of thankful praise. Some have understood verses 16–17 to state absolutely that God does not want ritual sacrifice, but a more qualified interpretation seems suitable. For such deliberate and extensive sins as are confessed in this psalm, ritual expiations were not thought adequate. Hope rested only in God's grace, appealed to by one truly penitent, 'broken' and 'crushed' in heart and spirit – the opposite of the arrogant heart of the rebellious sinner. Verses 18–19 are often considered a later addition, made while Jerusalem was in ruins. Reacting to the thought of verses 16–17, the addition would affirm that when the walls are rebuilt, God will again accept the offerings favourably. However, if the singer has a representative capacity, he can well conclude his penitential psalm with the prayer of verse 18; this prayer for the 'building' of the walls will refer to their strengthening, repairing and prospering through divine care. Verse 19 then implies a vow: when the atonement which can only be made by repentance and grace is effected, leader and community will offer sacrifices, costly and in abundance, in thanksgiving for the restoration of right relationship or fellowship.

The singer utters all the penitence and longing of an individual heart, but in a way that lets the assembly enter into his prayer, both one by one and as a group. All the wrong-doing is focused as *an alienation from God*. And from this most miserable condition God alone, in his faithfulness, grace, tender love and pity, can deliver. So the supplication rises for his thorough washing, purifying, creating, renewing of the whole person in the springs of thought, being and action. Led by the psalm into profound penitence, trusting in the one offering that fulfils all sacrifice, Christians to this day turn again to the Lord who creates and re-creates, while the visible sacraments still convey the deep purposes of his grace.

Gracious Lord, grant us true penitence, that you may be pleased to wash us from our sins and make our hearts anew; and take not your holy Spirit from us, that our tongue may ever sing of your goodness.

❦ Psalm 56 ❦

Tears Treasured in Heaven

1   *Be gracious to me, God, for man tramples over me,*
     all day long fighting and pressing upon me.
2   *My foes trample over me all the day;*
     many are those that fight against me, O Most High.
3   *Yet in the day when I fear,*
     I will put my trust in you.
4   *In God whose word I praise, in God I trust and will not fear;*
     for what can flesh do to me?
5   *All the day long they wound with words;*
     their every thought is to do me harm.
6   *They band together and lie in wait,*
     watching my heels as they eagerly seek my life.
7   *Shall they escape for all their wickedness?*
     In anger bring the peoples down, O God.
8   *You have counted all my groans,*
         my tears are laid up in your bottle;
     are they not noted in your book?
9   *If my enemies turn back on the day when I call,*
     then shall I know that God is with me.
10 *In God whose word I praise,*
     in the Lord whose word I praise,
11 *in God I trust and will not fear;*
     for what can man do to me?
12 *Gladly will I render the vows to you;*
     fully will I bring you the offerings of thanksgiving.
13 *For you will deliver my soul from death*
         and my feet from falling,
     to walk before God in the light of life.

Although the psalmist seems to speak as an individual, 'trampled' by
enemies, assailed by cruel words, in danger from lurkers who are

eager for his life, a national dimension appears in the expressions for the foes. These are warring and numerous, peoples or nations. So the sufferer can be well understood to be a king, bearing in his own soul hostilities against his land and nation from other peoples. He appeals to God to bring down the pride of human armies, and he especially praises the 'word' or covenant-promises to the dynasty. He looks forward to serving in peace before the face of God, in all the abundant light and life granted to the Lord's Anointed.

1–4 The lamented situation may be the raiding of territory by foreign enemies; it is as though they trampled on the king's own person. The frequency of the attacks, the great number of the assailants, here are details that call for God's speedy help. Professions of trust also give point to the appeal – how could such a one be disappointed? God's 'word', the sum of his commitments and promises, is praised as wholly trustworthy.

5–11 As often, it is malevolent words which the psalmist laments. They are words meant to bring ruin, and in ancient warfare they might take the form of ritual cursing and deceitful propaganda. The ambushes may have been a reality, especially for outlying populations, attacks which the king feels in his own person. The prayer is that the aggressive peoples should be 'brought down' – down from their pride, down to the dust. Verse 8 refers to the mourning, penitential style of the national intercession; the Lord will have seen the extent of the king's abasement – his lamenting gestures and sighs, the many tears he has shed. Indeed God does not despise such tears, but as it were treasures them up in a heavenly water-skin as precious signs of penitence and faith.

12–13 The singer willingly undertakes responsibility for the community's thank-offerings when deliverance shall be given, and he promises they will be brought in full, without stinting. He will give praise and testimony for the salvation that will have delivered him and his community from death and the abyss, and enabled him to serve once more in the presence of God, the source of light and life.

Against the wounding words and thoughts, our psalmist sets the word of God. Praising that word, he is enabled to trust and to cast out fear, perceiving the emptiness of human might in comparison with the power of God. At the same time he brings his grief to God, and penitence for sins; and he knows that every tossing of a supplicant's head, and every tear, is taken up and treasured by God, who does not despise the broken heart. Feeling in his own soul the suffering of vulnerable people that are daily trampled on, he is a type of all true pastors, a prefiguration indeed of Christ who 'offered up prayers and supplications with loud cries and tears' (Hebrews 5.5f).

Defend us, O God, from the false words of man by your eternal Word; and may the tears and prayers of Jesus deliver our souls from death and our feet from falling, that we may walk before you in the light of his eternal life.

Psalm 60

Trouble like an Earthquake

1   O God, you have spurned us and thrown us down;
      you were angry – O restore us anew.
2   You made the earth shudder and rent it apart;
      heal its wounds, for it is shaking.
3   You have filled your people with a bitter drink;
      you have given us a wine that makes us stagger.
4   You have made those who fear you flee,
      to escape from the reach of the bow.   [Pause]
5   That your beloved may be delivered,
      save by your right hand and answer us.
6   God has spoken in his holiness:
         In triumph I will portion out Shechem,
      and share out the valley of Sukkoth.
7   Mine shall be Gilead, and mine Manasseh;
      Ephraim shall be my helmet, and Judah my sceptre.
8   But Moab shall be my wash-bowl;
         over Edom I will throw my sandal;
      acclaim me, O Philistia!
9   Who will bring me to the fortress city;
      who could lead me up to Edom?
10   Have you not spurned us, O God,
      and will you not go out with our hosts?
11   O grant us help against the enemy,
      for earthly help is in vain.
12   Through God we can do mighty things;
      it is he that will tread down our foes.

Military defeat here occasions lamenting supplication, expressed partly as the voice of the people and partly as that of king or other leader (v.9). The psalm is distinctive in containing also an answering word of God, greeted with renewed supplication. While confrontations with the Edomites (v.9) were not uncommon, this fits best in the royal period when there was still a national army. In the urgent circumstances of war, such intercession may have taken place at a mobile altar on campaign rather than at the temple.

1–5 Prayer for restoration and salvation is accompanied with a vivid picture of the people's plight. It is all put as the result of God's anger. To judge from later verses, the language of earthquake is not meant literally, but expresses the sense that their world has collapsed; not actual buildings have been demolished, nor has the earth been made to quake and split, and left with fissures and aftershocks. But severe defeat has demolished morale and shaken the ground of their existence. The Lord has given them a cup of judgement to drink, and they stagger almost senseless from its force. The people are depicted as faithful worshippers, fearing God and beloved by him.

6–8 To the prayer 'answer us' comes a response, a word of God. The psalmist may have the prophetic gift both to intercede and to mediate answers from God. Or it may be that the oracle comes through another voice (as in the case of 2 Chronicles 20.14f). The picturesque oracle may have been a traditional one from the early days of David's kingdom. It is cited now to affirm that God remains sovereign over the holy land and still supports his people. In triumphant song, God depicts himself as a conqueror sharing out territory both east and west of the Jordan (Sukkot on the east, Shechem on the west). For himself he takes Gilead on the east, and the tribal areas chiefly on the west – Manasseh, Ephraim and the southerly Judah. The intention may be to mention representative and core areas, not least the rich and central Ephraim and the royal Judah, home of David. Surrounding lands are then mentioned as also owned by God, no longer hostile, but subdued. Moab's role, by comparison with that of Ephraim and Judah, seems a lowly one; the image of God's 'wash-bowl' may have been suggested by the striking views as one looks east from the Judean hills, the line of Moab's mountains forming a misty rim above the vivid blue waters of the Dead Sea. The sandal cast over Edom betokens God's ownership and lordship. The note of subjection in these images is understandable in a context of warring neighbours, but with the main idea of a united kingdom under God there is hidden a seed of peace and amity.

9–12   It seems that the defeat has been suffered in war with Edom in the southern mountains, and part of the oracle will have spoken directly to this calamity. But the triumphant mood of the old poem must have seemed a long way from the present dismay. The response of king and people therefore begins tactfully in question form: will God really lead me successfully through and up the formidable cliffs of Edom, whose capital city is virtually inaccessible? A blunter question follows: Have you not spurned us and deserted our armies? The conclusion asks again for God's salvation, owning that human help alone is useless.

Disaster has struck the worshippers of the Lord like an earthquake. Their world, it seems has fallen about them. The ground beneath them has parted, and still sways ominously. They lament that God has given them a cup of destiny that has sent them staggering. Their petitions are short gasps: 'Restore us, save us.' An answer comes, but one that takes them back to the beginning of the life in the holy land. They hear again the joyful song of the Lord, as he was set to establish his kingdom there, with happiness and strength for his people. Resounding again, the song means that God's purpose still stands, defeat will be overcome, the enemy subdued. This message, however, is received with some reserve. It has not actually referred to the present affliction, and the old vision of glory only points up the present misery and dismay, though the psalmist's last words are of trust and hope.

All through history there have been such situations. In tragic circumstances, believers can be reminded of God's classic promises and purposes, but may wonder all the more how they are to ascend from their present depths to the strong city and the lofty goal. The psalm would have them listen afresh to the old oracles, the promises, the gospel of the kingdom; and though, as prayer is renewed, doubts still linger, yet the sense of the only true help will grow. The wounded earth will come to be known as his possession, and his beloved will be led over every rock and chasm to his city of salvation.

O Lord Jesus, the conqueror of evil, help us in all our troubles to hear afresh your gospel words; that our faith may be rekindled, and by your Spirit we may do mighty deeds of love.

A Cry from the End of the Earth

1   Hear my crying, O God,
     and listen to my prayer.
2   From the end of the earth I call to you with fainting heart;
     lead me up the rock that is too high for me.
3   For you shall be a shelter for me,
     a strong tower against the foe.
4   May I dwell in your tent for ever,
     and shelter in the covering of your wings.   [Pause]
5   For you, O God, will hear my vows;
     you will grant the request of those who fear your name.
6   You will add days to the days of the king,
     that his years may be throughout all generations.
7   May he dwell before God for ever;
     bid faithful love and truth to guard him.
8   So shall I ever make music to your name,
     day by day fulfilling my vows.

A special feature of this supplication is that in verses 6–7 the prayer is explicitly for the king and in the third person. There are several indications in the other verses also that the supplicant is a king. The nature of the danger is not made clear; the 'enemy' may be of military character.

1–5   Prayer rises from a dire situation. The 'end of the earth' is the experience of being almost gone from light and life. The 'heart' has almost lost all strength, and the supplicant can only cry to the Lord to lead him from the dark waters up to the 'rock' of safety, which he cannot reach alone. 'Rock' suggests the holy mountain, or even God himself; he indeed will be a shelter and high tower for his king against 'the enemy', the forces of evil. And the prayer is supported by reference to the far-reaching vows of service when life is restored and to the prayer of all the loyal people.

6–8   The theme of the desired royal blessings continues – to dwell close to God, to have the guardian angels of faithful love and truth, and most characteristic of all, life 'for ever', 'throughout all generations'. The third person reference to the king may be a clue that a choir sings verses 6–7, expressing the people's 'request' just mentioned; or it may simply be a matter of style, and bringing out the hopes associated with the royal calling. With the offerings will sound the psalm-songs of testimony and thanksgiving, and they will especially praise the holy name in which the power and presence, the grace and salvation of the Lord are made known to his king.

In this prayer from 'the end of the earth', the extremity of human endurance, there come to expression the hopes based on God's promises to his king – the salvation found in the mighty rock, high above the evil tides; the safety in the embrace of the divine mother-love; the constant care of the angels that represent the divine faithfulness; eternal life in the home of God. In the ancient world, the expression of such hopes for the royal soul was not meant to exclude the general people. They found light and breath in their king (2 Samuel 21.17; Lamentations 4.20); the blessings focused on him were yet of benefit to all. So their 'request' for him, made in the fear and faith of God, was an act of solidarity. They would make with him the ascent on the great rock of God.

Likewise in the church's use of this psalm, the worshippers cry with Christ from the edge of endurance, from the mouth of the abyss. With him they ascend the rock which they cannot climb alone; with him they dwell with the Father. Day by day they offer their lives, and make music to praise the name by which they have been given true life.

Father, hear us when we pray from the limits of our endurance; and as you brought up your Son Jesus, so lead us upon your rock, to abide with you for ever in praise and thanksgiving.

Psalm 62

Secrets of Stillness

1   For God alone my soul waits in stillness;
    from him comes my salvation.
2   He only is my rock and my salvation,
    my stronghold, so that I shall not be utterly shaken.
3   How long will you assault a man, all of you intent to destroy,
    as you would a leaning wall or damaged defence?
4   They consult only how to thrust me from my height,
        and have delighted in falsehood;
    they blessed with their mouth,
        but in their heart they cursed.   [Pause]
5   To God alone be still, my soul;
    from him comes all my hope.
6   He alone is my rock and my salvation,
    my stronghold, so that I shall not be shaken.
7   In God is my salvation and my glory;
    my mighty rock and my refuge is God.
8   Trust in him always, O people;
    pour out your heart before him,
        for God is our refuge.   [Pause]
9   The children of earth are but a breath, the peoples a delusion;
    on the scales they all are lighter than air.
10 Do not trust in oppression or be deluded by plunder;
    if power abounds, give it no regard.
11 Once has God declared it,
    twice have I heard the same,
    that power belongs to God,
12 and yours, Lord, is faithful love.
    For you yourself reward everyone
    according to their deeds.

The psalmist faces opponents who would thrust him from his eminence; they are like an assaulting army that has damaged a city wall and now moves in to bring it down. The indications, therefore, are that a king is under attack, threatened in his eminent position above his people and as their wall of defence. The general tone is of trust, and this amounts to an indirect appeal to God – may he vindicate this trust declared so openly and repeatedly.

1–4 The opening is immediately a statement of trust in 'God alone', the only source of salvation. Towards him the soul 'is stillness' (so the Hebrew literally), acknowledging that it is God's action that will be decisive, and opening the way for it. The appeal to God is indirect in this statement of trust. And likewise the lament depicting the danger is conveyed indirectly through an address to the enemies, who are then described. It seems that there have been outward courtesies, only concealing plots to oust him from his position of eminence. The hostility of the enemies in fact is felt as a continuous assault to destroy him; some insecurity or weakness in his position spurs them on to finish his downfall.

5–10 As though to counter the disturbing portrayal of the enemies, the psalmist resumes his opening testimony of trust, but with a significant heightening. It is now an exhortation to his soul, in defiance of the alarming situation, to be still before God; and additional statements of trust in God's protection are made in verse 7. Then in verse 8 the address turns to the people. They are the psalmist's loyal people, who with him should trust in the protection God has promised. It seems they are in danger of being overawed, even seduced, by the enemy's power, with all its violence and ill-gotten wealth. Such human might, counsels the psalmist, is a delusion, nothing to weigh against the power of God. They should 'pour out' their heart before God, unburdening themselves of anxieties and counsels of despair, confessing all their weakness, allowing him to make them a pure and steadfast heart.

11–12 In conclusion, the fundamental theme – God the only hope – is repeated as counsel for the people and for his own soul, and as a pleading testimony before God. Now, however, it is presented in another aspect – as revelation, spoken frequently by the mouth of God himself, and so of the utmost solemnity and reliability. 'Once ... twice': such mounting numbers in the ancient poetry indicate numerous occurrences; this was the burden of many oracles given to king and people, that their salvation was in his might, faithful love, and justice.

What a contrast between the battering assault of the enemy and the stillness of the soul towards God! It is precisely because of the acute danger, and indeed the beginnings of disaster, that the theme of trust is sung out with such emphasis and repetition in this psalm. The singer has to contend not only with a conspiracy of foes determined to bring him crashing down from his eminence and glory, but also with his own people's temptation to change sides, in view of the enemy's power and growing success. His testimony to salvation in God alone is made to strengthen his own soul, to fortify and guide his people, and implicitly to appeal to God to vindicate the declarations of trust.

There are 'deeds' enough (v.12) from all the human participants in this drama – activity of self-defence on the one hand, conspiracy, treachery, lies and plunder on the other; and in the midst of it all the psalmist finds a stillness towards God. Before the almighty Lord, his soul is a still centre. And the meaning of this silence of the spirit is trust – profound and decisive acknowledgement that power belongs to God, and in him alone is salvation; he is faithful, and the source of all true hope. Perhaps it is on the way to this stillness that the wavering people are counselled to 'pour out' their heart before God. As they lay all their fears and doubts at his feet, they too will be granted that stillness which is the best prayer for the mighty deeds of the Saviour.

O God, in whom alone is our hope and salvation, help us amid all the blows of life to confess to you our failures and fears; and help us to pour out our hearts before you, until we find that stillness where we are sure that you alone will make all things well.

⤳ Psalm 65 ⤳

For the dear Earth

1   Praise is hushed for you, O God, in Zion,
    and for you the vow is fulfilled, you that answer prayer.
2   To you come all the children of earth, confessing wrongs;
3   though our sins prevailed against us,
        you have purged them away.
4   Happy the one you choose and bring near
        to dwell in your courts;
    we shall be satisfied with the goodness of your house,
        your holy temple.
5   With dread deeds in justice you will answer us,
        O God of our salvation,
    O hope of all the ends of the earth
        and the sea where the Far Ones dwell,
6   you that set fast the mountains by your might,
    having girded on your strength,
7   who stilled the raging of the seas,
    the roar of their waves, and the tumult of the peoples.
8   Those who dwell at the farthest bounds
        trembled at your wonders;
    the gates of morning and evening sang your praise.
9   O tend the earth and water her, and greatly enrich her;
    with the heavenly stream full of water
        you will prepare her corn,
        yes, so you will prepare her.
10 Soak well her furrows and settle her ridges;
    soften her with showers, and bless her springing.
11 O crown a year of your bounty,
    and let your tracks flow down with goodness.
12 May the pastures of the wilderness flow with your goodness,
    and the hills be girded with joy.
13 May the fields be clothed with flocks,
    and the valleys stand so thick with corn,
        that they shall laugh and sing.

❧❧❧

In festal assembly at Zion, the community prays for God to send the vital rains, and so prepare a year of good growth and harvests. After introductory praise and acknowledgment of God's mighty deeds of creation (vv.1–8), thought turns to the present need for creation's renewal – God's saturation of the earth, his inauguration of a year of his bounty, his preparation for abundant flocks and corn. The festival will be that of the autumn, when the new agricultural cycle was about to begin, but where ceremonies had to include fulfilment of vows of thank-offerings and confession and atonement of sin.

1–4   The tumultuous acclamation of God dies away. A quiet awe of his nearness prevails at the time of sacrifice. The vow of sacrifice made in time of need is fulfilled at the festival, with testimony to the faithful God who answered the prayer. For 'all flesh', all the human race especially, only God can truly grant expiation of sins that are too strong for them alone. The psalm is probably not prophesying here some future transformation when 'all flesh shall come', but rather expressing the present ideal of God manifest in Zion as Creator and ruler of all. The element of atonement will always have been an important aspect of this festal season, a fundamental part of the theme of renewal for individuals, people, and world. But within that universal work of the Creator, those actually gathered in the temple courts, so near to the holy manifestation, were conscious of a special grace. They attribute their peculiar happiness to the gracious will of God, who has chosen each of them and brought them into the very aura of his sanctuary-presence, to drink deeply of his holy fountain of life.

5–8   Prayer is now raised that God will answer the worshippers' cry for rains and all that earth needs in her new cycle of life. By 'dread deeds in righteousness' is meant a renewal of the mighty work by which he first founded life and healthful order. The recital of these mighty deeds (vv.6–8) is indirectly a prayer for their renewal – making firm earth's mountain-pillars, subduing the waters to serve life (the stilling of rebellious peoples is part of the Creator's work in his ongoing rule). The universality of his work is emphasized by reference to the involvement of the farthest bounds of the world. Dwellers at the world's edge, indeed the very gates of light on the horizon in farthest east and west, responded to the work of creation with awe and praise.

9–13 The Creator is implored to soak the land, at present parched from the long summer drought. The rains may fail in Palestine, and starvation and impoverishment were well-known experiences. The prayers and ceremonies of the autumn festal were so much the more earnest. The poet here beautifully expresses the marvel of good rains, which lead the barren earth through the orderly stages of cultivation and growth, until the hillsides and valleys are clad with crops and healthy flocks, themselves appearing to laugh and sing for joy in God.

How profound the happiness that God in grace has brought this people to his house at this time! They are replenished in the springs of life, quickened by the light of his holy presence. From a people so 'brought near', cleansed and renewed, a great prayer then arises: may this God, this mighty Creator who formed and ordered the vast cosmos, may he renew his mighty deeds and grant a year blessed with his gifts of life. The prayer is full of sympathy for the good earth and her needs, which God will lovingly attend to. And there is warm feeling too for the hills and valleys that will wear the garments of praise, the clothing of green and gold, and contented flocks and herds.

The cycle of growth and the life it supported were precarious. The ancient worshippers felt that all was in the hands of the mighty Creator, and happiness was to be right with him and near to him. So the fields and flocks would be bound in the circle of blessing, and the prayer of life would be heard. But can the song from the gates of morning and evening still be heard, the trust of farthest spaces still be known? Yes, surely it will be so, when the secret of worship is grasped.

O God, whose work of creation embraces all that exists, grant us to know what it is to be brought near to dwell in your courts; cleanse and replenish our souls, that our prayer for the earth may be a song in tune with the trust of the distant seas and the music of the gates of morning and evening.

Psalm 67

For the Blessing of Earth

1   *May God be gracious to us and bless us,*
    and make his face to shine on our path,   *[Pause]*
2   *that your way may be known on earth,*
    your salvation among all nations.
3   *Then the peoples will praise you, O God;*
    yes, all the peoples will praise you.
4   *The nations will rejoice and sing,*
    that you govern the peoples justly,
      and guide the nations on earth.
5   *The peoples will praise you, O God;*
    yes, all the peoples will praise you.
6   *May earth give her increase.*
    May God, our God, grant us his blessing.
7   *May God give us his blessing,*
    that all the ends of the earth may fear him.

Verse 6 is best translated as referring to the future: 'Earth shall give . . .' or 'May earth give her increase'. The psalm will then be a prayer of the community for rains and good growth, the divine blessings that alone sustain life.

1–2   Prayer is raised that God should act in grace and goodwill – that his face should give light or shine towards his creatures; the literal here is to shine 'with us', the sense being perhaps that his presence and power should ever assist the worshippers on their path. That he should 'bless' means especially that he should grant healthy life and increase, not least by sending good rains. It is characteristic of this psalm that the worshippers see such blessing, and all the good rule of God, as for all the world. His 'way' may mean here his path as he moves through the earth in his mighty work to provide for life. 'Salvation' here involves God's conquest of chaos and his securing of life.

3–5 The thought continues in its universal scope. Rather than a vow of praise from the Israelites, there is declaration that all earth's peoples will give thanks for such salvation, rejoicing in the good reign of God. The theme is emphasized with much repetition, and serves to add strength to the supplication for blessing.

6–7 It becomes clear now that the desired blessing concerns especially the good things for life that earth 'gives', the plants that grow for man and beast. For these indeed there will be thankful worship of the Creator across all the world, with awe at his power and goodness.

The sight and sound of strong rain made the people of the psalms think directly of blessing from heaven. The rising green of earth told of the shining face of God, bright with favour. Good crops and flocks and herds spoke of his passing though the earth, the victor over chaos, the Creator who wrought the miracle of life. But the joy of all the earth was to be not so much in the gifts themselves, as in him, the saviour, 'God, our God'. The glad song was a thanksgiving, a testimony to the ruler and guide of all creation. And to him, at every stage of the year's growth, prayer was raised, as to the one who alone could so give and sustain life. The psalm thus summons to deep reflection a generation that sees cultivation as only a matter for human science and economic power.

Creator and Saviour of the world, grant us in our generation to know that we live only by the light of your face, and flourish only through the pouring down of your blessing; may we respect the good earth, and value all that you enable her to give, until all peoples fear your majesty and sing to you the song of thanksgiving.

The Saviour King

1   O God, give your judgements to the king,
      your justice to this son of the king.
2   Then he shall judge your people aright,
      and your afflicted ones with justice.
3   The mountains shall bear peace,
      and the little hills goodness for the people.
4   He shall judge for the poor of the people;
      he will save the children of the needy,
         and crush the oppressor.
5   He shall prolong his years with the sun,
      and before the moon, for all generations.
6   He shall come down like rain on the crops,
      like showers that water the earth.
7   In his days shall justice flourish,
      and abundance of peace, till the moon be no more.
8   And he shall rule from sea to sea,
      and from the great river to the ends of the earth.
9   Wild creatures shall kneel before him,
      but his enemies shall lick the dust.
10   The kings of Tarshish and the isles shall give presents;
      the kings of Arabia and Saba will bring gifts.
11   And all kings shall bow down before him,
      all nations do him service.
12   For he shall deliver the poor one who cries out,
      the needy one who has no helper.
13   He will have pity on the helpless and needy,
      and save the lives of the poor.
14   From falsehood and cruelty he will redeem their soul,
      and their blood shall be precious in his eyes.
15   So they shall live, and bring him more than Arabia's gold,
      as they pray for him continually,
         and bless him all the day long.

16 *The corn shall be abundant on the earth and hill-tops,*
        its fruit heavy as on Lebanon.
     and from their cities they will flourish
        as the grass of the earth.
17 *His name shall live for ever,*
        and continue as long as the sun;
     all nations shall bless themselves by him,
        and call him blessed.
18 *Blessed be the Lord God, God of Israel,*
     who alone does wonderful things;
19 *and blessed be his glorious name for ever,*
     and may all the earth be filled with his glory. Amen and amen.

This prayer and prophetic blessing for the king has such a fundamental and idealistic character, that it probably belonged to the ceremonies of royal installation, and perhaps also to services of renewal. By prayer and prophetic word, the king is to become a true channel of the heavenly justice, above all defending the poor and vulnerable; and then will follow heaven's gifts to the land, and indeed the whole earth – a harmony of nature, health and abundance.

1–4 The whole psalm flows from the prayer of verse 1. This asks God, understood as the true king of all, to enact his just rule through the human king who is his viceroy and chief servant. The 'judgements' are more than legal decisions; they embrace all the work of government, but especially the care of the poor. The king is also referred to as 'son of (the) king', an expression equivalent to 'king' and so meaning the Davidic heir, the dynastic representative. Undergirded by the opening prayer, the prospect of consequent blessing opens out. When the Davidic Son is truly the channel of God's rule, these wonderful things will follow. God's people will be ruled with honesty and fairness; the afflicted, lowly, poor and needy will be helped and defended, and oppressors crushed. Such rightness of rule is seen as one with the good order God wills for all the world of life. The 'peace' and 'rightness' borne by the hills mean good crops and fruit, but as part of a total harmony of society and nature.

5–11   The long life for the king can be understood of dynastic continuance, but as it stands it expresses the ideal of a ruler wholly true to God in his compassionate justice – such a ruler would live and reign for ever. In such a vision of the ideal, the psalm is profoundly related to the later hope of a Messiah. The wonder of such a prospect is further developed. The effect on the natural world is resumed from verse 3. The king enabled by God to be thus just and compassionate would be like good rains bringing good harvests, and again 'rightness' and 'peace' comprehend the health and happiness of both nature and society. The seas and 'river' of verse 8 are probably forms of the cosmic waters that surround and penetrate the earth. In verse 9, 'wild creatures' are desert animals, and their kneeling or crouching before the truly just king is again a sign of harmony in creation. Former enemies will come to make lowly obeisance before him, kings from afar bring gifts and tribute (Tarshish represents the far west, perhaps Tartessus in Spain; 'Saba' may be along the coasts of the Red Sea).

12–17   All this glory is for the king who is the channel of God's justice, and its focus – defence of the vulnerable and needy – is set out even more strongly than in verses 2 and 4. He will be their 'redeemer', alongside them as if his own nearest kin, holding their blood precious, and so ever eager to save them from hurt. Those that he so 'redeems' will then 'live' (restored to good life and freedom) and will give a better gift than the rich potentates offer, for they will pray for their king and bless him all the day long. With such a king, the fruits of the earth and the populations of towns will flourish and abound. The royal name and line will endure, to the blessing of all.

18–19   The psalm proper has ended, and now is added a typical formula of worship to round off the second 'book' of psalms (42–72). Such a blessing is the creatures' response to the Creator's blessing. It is all that, in the end, can be offered – fervent thanksgiving and praise.

The psalm can lead people of our times to hold up their rulers in prayer, that they may be mediators of divine goodness; that all their policies and decisions may flow from the great eternal justice, to defend the defenceless and to crush oppression; and to know that this is the path to the health and harmony of earth and all that lives in her.

Following from the insights of the Jewish interpreters, the church has also gained through the soaring poetry of the psalm a messianic vision. She has related it all to Jesus, Messiah and mediator of God's reign, and prayed that his work for the helpless and for the restoration of the world of goodness and peace may come to full fruition. And there is also an application of this great prayer to each disciple, for each one in Christ becomes a channel of the divine compassion and justice in their own realm of influence, and each comes down there like rain to the crops and helps restore earth's peace. The people of the church can well join in the concluding 'Amen and Amen'. For they give thanks that in answer to all the prayers of this book of psalms there has been given the vision of the Messiah and kingdom of the Lord, where the poor find true life, the wild creatures come to their Saviour, and earth has her springing of God's peace and goodness.

O God, eternal King, who caused the hope for the Messiah to arise, and answered it in your Son Jesus, we bless you for his care of the needy, and for the peace and salvation which he brings to those who love him; and we ask that his work be completed, and all the earth be filled with your glory; Amen and Amen.

Drawing Near to God

1   Truly God is good to Israel,
    to those who are pure in heart.
2   But as for me, my feet were almost gone;
    my steps had all but slipped.
3   For I was envious of the proud;
    I saw the prosperity of the wicked.
4   For them there are no sharp pains;
    their body is well and fat.
5   The common sufferings are not for them;
    they are not smitten like other folk.
6   Therefore pride is their necklace,
    and cruelty covers them like a garment.
7   Their iniquity comes from within them;
    the conceits of their heart overflow.
8   They scoff and speak only evil;
    they pronounce oppression from on high.
9   They stretch their mouth to the heavens,
    and their tongue licks through the earth.
10 So their people gather round them,
    and drink in their doctrine to the full.
11 And they say, How should God know it?
    Is there knowledge in the Most High?
12 See, such are the wicked,
    and being ever at ease, they increase their wealth.
13 Did I then cleanse my heart in vain,
    and wash my hands in innocence?
14 All day long have I been stricken,
    and every morning chastened anew.
15 But if I had said, I will speak thus,
    I should have betrayed the company of your children.
16 When I thought to understand this,
    it seemed too hard for me,

17   *until I came into the sanctuary of God;*
     and then I discerned their end.

18   *For you will set them in slippery places,*
     and make them fall to destruction.

19   *O how suddenly they will come to ruin,*
     be overcome by terrors and perish!

20   *As when one awakes from a dream,*
     so, Lord, when you arise, you will dispel their image.

21   *When I was bitter in heart,*
     and consumed with grief within me,

22   *I was but simple and ignorant,*
     even as a beast before you.

23   *But I am always with you;*
     you keep hold of my right hand.

24   *You will guide me with your counsel,*
     and afterwards receive me in glory.

25   *Whom have I in heaven but you?*
     And there is none that I desire on earth beside you.

26   *My flesh and my heart shall fail;*
     but God is the rock of my heart and my portion for ever.

27   *Those who go far from you shall perish;*
     you will silence those who forsake you for false gods.

28   *But it is good for me to draw near to God;*
     in the Lord God I will make my shelter,
         that I may tell of all your works.

❦

It may be best to see the psalmist as throughout concerned with what he calls 'drawing near to God' (v.28). In a time of suffering, both personal and national, he seeks shelter, communion, and reviving grace in the sanctuary. Much of the psalm is then a kind of preparation, a meditation and confession, composing the heart for communion and trustfully resting an agonizing situation in the hands of the Lord.

The arrogant and flourishing troublers described at such length may be foreign tyrants of great power, in contrast to the suffering people. The psalmist appears to represent and be responsible for the latter (v.15), and several phrases suggest he is the king – clasped by God's right hand, led by his counsel, taken to glory.

1 The beginning and conclusion of the psalm are like a frame enclosing the account of doubt and reviving faith. However it may seem, God is indeed loving and gracious to his faithful people. The 'pure in heart' here makes clear that 'Israel' is understood as the people sincerely devoted to God. A concern with injustice between nations is already apparent; the psalmist has been wrestling with the problem of his nation's suffering.

2–14 He now begins a confession of foolishness, which almost led to a fatal fall from God. Bitter indignation welled up when he saw how the arrogant prospered in comfort, while he himself, taking God's way in innocence, was continually afflicted. The extended description of the wicked serves to keep them exposed to the divine judgment; there seems to be an implicit appeal for action. The oppressors are typified as wealthy folk become proud and insensitive. They have leisure to devise evil, and they grasp and devour far and wide. Because of their power they are admired and emulated. Their attitude is that a just God can be left out of the reckoning.

15 One consideration helped to steady the sliding feet. The psalmist knew he must not betray the 'generation' or 'congregation' of God's children. It seems that he had a prominent responsibility. The people of the Lord looked to him and drew strength of faith from him. From this solidarity he too was strengthened.

16–20 But still the aggravation was a sore burden; to his eyes it was all perplexity and grief. Then relief came to him when he was in the temple. Through some enlightenment he saw how illusory was the stability of the wicked. Over them hung the threat of sudden ruin. He saw the certainty that God would act against them.

21–26 The psalmist confesses to God that it was through ignorance of his mystery that he had become so bitter, letting jealous indignation gnaw at his inward parts. But now he is renewed in the surpassing joy of the Lord's constant companionship and can affirm 'I am always with you'. God's hand-clasp expresses both his choice and support. Reference to the situation of God's king seems even clearer in verse 24. God's 'counsel' shows the way amid the problems of government. So guided, the Lord's Chosen One will at last be 'taken' or 'received' into glory. Although this could be understood of eventual victory on earth, a heavenly destiny is more probably in mind. And the psalmist affirms his loyalty to this Lord alone. In verse 26 some understand the failing of flesh and heart as a temporary suffering within earthly life; but the prospect could again be of an eternal bliss beyond the body's death.

27–28   In concluding appreciation of the blessing of nearness to God, the psalmist draws a contrast: forsaking God is the way to ruin, but 'drawing near' to God yields the supreme good, the divine shelter and salvation.

Through confession and meditation the way to draw near to God has been opened. To be always with God, to know the clasp of his hand, the salvation of his guidance and counsel through every peril, to be taken up at last into the glory of his nearer presence – these hopes begin to be realized. God becomes ever more surely 'rock of my heart, my portion for ever'.

   To what extent the psalmist may have looked beyond this life for the bliss of salvation remains disputed. Certainly he does not theorize about an afterlife. All the weight of hope is carried by the relationship with God. Given nearness to him, no other good is to be desired. As is further unfolded in the New Testament, eternal life is already bestowed on one who knows God. The failing of flesh and heart only makes clearer the true nature of that life as the enjoyment of God, 'my portion for ever' (John 6.54; 17.3).

Be our shelter, Lord God, in all the perplexities that assault our faith; guide us with your counsel, and bring us so close to you, that in this communion we come to know the fulfilment of all our hope and desire.

Prayer amid utter ruin

1   *Why, O God, have you so utterly rejected us,*
     why does your anger burn against the flock of your pasture?

2   *Remember your congregation which you purchased long ago,*
       and redeemed as the tribe for your own possession;
     remember the hill of Zion where you dwelt.

3   *Lift your steps to the utter ruins,*
     to all that the enemy has vilely done in the holy place.

4   *Your foes roared in the place for your worship;*
     instead of its signs they set up their standards.

5   *They were like woodmen with axes,*
     swinging them on high in a thicket of trees.

6   *And then her carved work altogether*
     they forced down with bars and hatchets.

7   *They set fire to your holy place;*
     to the very ground they defiled the dwelling of your name.

8   *They said in their heart, Let us crush them altogether;*
     they burnt all the sacred places in the land.

9   *There are no signs for us to see, and no longer any prophet,*
     not one among us, who knows how long.

10 *How long, O God, shall the adversary taunt,*
     and the enemy utterly revile your name?

11 *Why have you withdrawn your hand,*
     and held back your right hand in your bosom?

12 *O God, my King of ancient time,*
     who did deeds of salvation in the midst of earth,

13 *it was you that cleft the Sea by your power,*
     you that broke the dragons' heads on the waters.

14 *You alone crushed the heads of Leviathan;*
     you gave him as food for creatures of the desert.

15 *It was you that cleft fountain and river,*
     you that dried up ever-flowing rivers.

16 *From you came day, from you the night;*
     you alone established the sun and all the lights of heaven.

17   *It was you that set up all the edges of the earth,*
     you that fashioned both summer and winter.
18   *Remember, Lord, how the enemy derides,*
     how a foolish people scorns your name.
19   *Do not give to wild beasts the soul of your turtle-dove,*
     or forget the life of your suffering ones for ever.
20   *Look upon your covenant,*
          for the dark places of earth are filled;
     filled with victims are the fields of violence.
21   *May the oppressed not return ashamed,*
     but let the poor and needy praise your name.
22   *Arise, O God, take up your own cause;*
     remember how the fool reviles you all the day long.
23   *Do not forget the voice of your enemies,*
     the din of your foes that ascends continually.

The community here raises a lamenting supplication, pleading for God to exert his power in his own as well as his people's interest. The distress pictured in the lament centres on the devastation wrought by invaders in the sanctuary on Mount Zion; there are many dead, and instead of the daily offerings and praises it is the blasphemy of the foe that rises up to heaven. The most likely occasion was the conquest and destruction carried out by the Babylonians in 587 BCE. The psalm may have been voiced in lamenting worship which continued on the site of the ruined temple.

1–3   The intercessor at once begins to wrestle with the one who is Lord and shepherd of this people, and in whose will and power lies all their fate. The present disaster is not felt in the first place as caused by the enemy, but to be due to the Lord's displeasure with his people. So to this God, so personally conceived, is directly put the remonstrating question 'Why' and the urging to 'remember' the people he had once saved from oppression and made peculiarly his own, and also the mountain where, in the temple, he had 'dwelt' through the mystery of his name and glory. This 'presence' has been withdrawn, but let God lift up his steps, marching with martial purpose and speed, to intervene on this holy place, now in utter ruin.

4–11   The evil situation is now portrayed with the aim of stirring God's intervention. The focus, therefore, is on the appalling affront to his honour and majesty perpetrated by those who assailed his temple. They roared like lions in the pride of their strength; they put their military standards, connected with their gods, in place of the signs or symbols of the Lord's worship. With hatchets and crowbars they forced down the precious panels in the temple – of gold, ivory, fine wood – and then burnt it to ruins. Further, they burnt down every sacred place they could find in the land. With such disruption of the sacred orders, but even more because of God's wrath, no oracles or omens of hope are given. Neither prophets nor any other mediators can say when the turning will come. The lament is rounded off with the imploring questions, 'How long, O God . . . Why', and the situation is tellingly summarized – the enemy mocking God's name, and God unresponsive, his mighty right hand hidden and at rest in the folds of his garment.

12–17   In contrast to this right hand held back in the bosom, there follows an account of the mighty deeds it did in creation. The purpose of this recital is to beseech and indeed to move God to conquer the present manifestation of chaos. The imaginative poetry has its roots in ancient lore of creation stories evidenced among older Near-eastern peoples. For Israelite faith, it was the Lord who in the beginning established his kingly supremacy, vanquishing the monsters of chaos in direct combat. Such monsters were embodiments of the untamed, destructive waters, and the victory meant that these were now subdued, divided and made to serve the cosmos, the order of life. Chief of the monsters here was Leviathan (probably 'Twisting One'), with seven heads. From verse 15 the fundamental work of creation is followed further. The cleaving of fountain and river opened up passages down through the earth, evidencing the Lord's mastery over the water. By the same power were made the day and the night and all the lights of heaven. The last item of creation mentioned is the making of summer and winter. All has been recounted as what the Lord alone could and did achieve. Seven times the Hebrew uses the pronoun 'You (alone)' to sustain the emphasis; more than enough for the seven heads of chaos.

18–23 With a sharp change we are back to the present situation: 'Remember, Lord, how the enemy derides.' The suffering people is pictured as a turtle-dove once dear to God's heart but now cast to wild beasts. Only now does the depiction of suffering widen to count the human cost; the caverns and fields of the land of death are filled with the slain. The blasphemy of the enemies rises continually, where once the praises and continual offerings had ascended to heaven.

The scene reflected in the psalm is indeed very dark, for there was given as yet no word or sign of hope. But we know that the light of prophecy was in fact not far away. Through Jeremiah, Ezekiel and the Isaiah disciples (Isaiah 40f), meaning and hope would be re-discovered.

Still today it is utterly perplexing when the Creator holds back his right hand while his dove is cast to the beasts. Yet the church sees the cross as embodying all such agonies from beginning to end of time; to faith and silent contemplation its enigma becomes the greatest of all the revelatory signs.

God, who alone in your power established the world of life, look with pity upon your suffering ones and hasten to their help, as you raised the Lord Jesus from the fields of violence, to the glory of your Name for ever.

Psalm 77

The Intercessor's Strongest Plea

1   With my voice I cry to God,
      with all my voice to God, that he may hear me.

2   In the day of my trouble I seek the Lord;
      by night my hand is stretched out and does not tire,
         and my soul refuses to be comforted.

3   I think upon God and I groan;
      I ponder, and my spirit faints.   [Pause]

4   My eyelids are held open;
      I am so stricken that I cannot speak.

5   I consider the days of old,
      and remember the years of long ago.

6   I commune with my heart in the night;
      I ponder, and search my spirit.

7   Will the Lord for ever be spurning,
      will he not once again show favour?

8   Has his faithful love ceased for ever,
      and his promise come to an end for all generations?

9   Has God forgotten to be gracious,
      has he in anger shut up his compassion?   [Pause]

10   But I say, this shall be my entreaty:
      to recite the deeds of the right hand of God Most High.

11   I will celebrate the acts of the Lord;
      I will recall your wonders from of old.

12   I will recite all your work,
      and tell out all your deeds.

13   Your way, O God, was in holy splendour;
      what god is so great as the Lord?

14   You are the God who does marvels;
      you made known your power among the peoples.

15   With a mighty arm you redeemed your people,
      the children of Jacob and Joseph.   [Pause]

16   *The waters saw you, O God,*
      the waters saw you and trembled;
    and the depths also were shaken.
17   *The clouds poured out water, the skies uttered their thunder;*
    your arrows flashed on every side.
18   *The voice of your thunder was in the whirlwind,*
      your lightnings lit up the ground;
    earth trembled and shook with dread.
19   *Your way was in the sea,*
      and your paths through the great waters,
    and your footsteps were not known.
20   *You led your people like a flock,*
    by the hand of Moses and Aaron.

In this lamenting prayer, the singer tells of personal grief and distress, but it becomes clear that his concern is on behalf of his people. His recital of God's ancient deeds in the Exodus is an implied prayer for the renewal of such salvation; it is almost as if the prophetic intercessor calls the ancient deeds into present effect. The nation's ordeal seems to have been a protracted one, but is not clarified.

1–9   The lamenting entreaty is uttered to God with full voice, that he may indeed heed it. The singer portrays protracted distress to move the Lord – the hands stretched out in hours of supplication, the groaning of spirit night and day, the wakeful eyes, the force of grief, like a stroke that makes it hard to speak. It is perplexing to think of God's faithfulness of old; can he really have abandoned that enduring love, has he forgotten grace and compassion? Putting these sharp questionings in the form of a narrative, the intercessor avoids hurling them directly at God; but their force is unmistakable.

10   This rather ambiguous verse probably introduces the recital of praise, countering the preceding questions. The ancient work of God is to be recounted as plea for its renewal.

11–20   It is declared accordingly that the ancient miracles done by the Lord are now to be commemorated. It is the deliverance of the people from bondage in Egypt, the Exodus, which is recalled. The practical details are passed over; only the glory and wonder of God's action are mentioned, and their marvellous and life-giving nature is brought out by use of imagery drawn from traditions of Creation and the annual renewal of life. The waters are especially prominent because of their symbolizing chaos, destructive power which only the Creator masters and makes to serve life. Through the deepest waters trod the Saviour, where none could see his footprints, and so he came to rescue his flock, and tend them all through the wilderness through his servants Moses and Aaron. The abrupt ending is eloquent. The silence after verse 20 would itself be a moving entreaty. May the Holy One, whom deepest waters cannot hold back, come again to save his people.

The psalm is an example of the strenuous work of the intercessors. Taking all the trouble of their people upon themselves and into their own heart, they cry for them to the Lord with outstretched hands and grieving soul; and through many an hour they ponder deeply on the absence of God's help. Their entreaty finds its full force as they address to God the recollection of his ancient salvation, the foundation of present life and hope. In the silence that follows, the voiceless prayer for renewal of that work of love rises with inspired strength. It is surely heard, though the Saviour's footsteps through the deep waters of sorrow are not known.

Lord, who can come through the deepest waters to rescue your suffering ones, strengthen those who watch and suffer in prayer for others; inspire them to grasp with faith the salvation which gave birth to your world and your people, and to rest their plea upon it.

Psalm 84

Travelling to God

1   How lovely is your dwelling,
    almighty Lord of Hosts!

2   My soul longed and fainted for the courts of the Lord;
    my heart and my flesh cried out for the living God.

3   But now the bird has found her home, the swallow her nest,
    where she may lay her young near your altars,
        Lord of Hosts, my King and my God.

4   Happy those who dwell in your house,
    for they are ever praising you.   [Pause]

5   Happy those whose strength comes from you,
    for the ascent to your house is in their heart.

6   Passing through the driest valley,
        they make it a place of springs,
    and the autumn rain will cover it with blessings.

7   They will go from strength to strength,
    until they see the God of Gods in Zion.

8   Lord God of Hosts, hear my prayer;
    give heed, O God of Jacob.   [Pause]

9   Look with favour on our shield, O God;
    regard the face of your Anointed.

10   Better indeed a day in your courts,
    than any thousand I could choose.

11   Better to touch but the threshold of the house of my God,
    than to abide in the tents of wickedness.

12   For the Lord is both sun and shield, giving grace and glory;
    the Lord will not withhold good from those who walk in truth.

13   O Lord of Hosts,
    happy the one who trusts in you.

Praise of God fills much of this psalm, though expressed indirectly through appreciation of his sanctuary on Zion and the communion

which he grants there. The thoughts of the psalm make it probable
that it expressed praise and prayer at the outset of the festal
celebrations in the autumn. A singer, representative of the great
assembly, catches the spirit of pilgrims on their journey and their
satisfaction on arrival, and so fittingly leads them all in a
fundamental prayer for the king, the Lord's Anointed, the channel
of God's blessings.

1–3 Praise is expressed in an exclamation of wonder, which
reflects the emotion of pilgrims who have come across the hilly
country from their villages and towns and at last see the beauty of
the holy city and temple. The depth of the love and joy is in the
knowledge that here is the abode of the almighty Lord of Hosts, the
'living God'; it is the place where the Lord of all creation receives
his worshippers and bestows on them new life. On behalf of the
pilgrims, the singer recalls that sense of longing and need far from
the holy place and time, the weariness and thirst that cried out for
the fountain of life. But now the pilgrim soul has come with deep
satisfaction to her true home; she is the swallow that nests happily in
the peace of the sanctuary.

4–7 The praise now takes the form of declaring the good fortune
of those who enjoy the communion God grants in worship at his
sanctuary. First are mentioned those who 'dwell' in the holy place –
the sacred ministers, from the king, priests and musicians to the
humble cleaners and porters. All these servants of the household of
the Lord have constant opportunity to praise him in that blessed
place of his name and presence. But there is a special happiness also
given to the pilgrims, and this is dwelt on at some length. Already in
the preparation and beginning of their journey (v.5), when the final
ascent up the holy hill is still only a longed-for goal in heart and
imagination, they begin to be touched by the Lord's grace, and
receive from him strength to face the difficulties and persevere.
Then they are pictured in mid-course. Some particular valley, noted
for its dryness, represents the hot and dusty route before the long
summer drought is broken. How dead everything seems! But the
pilgrims keep hope, holding to the Lord's power to work the miracle
of transformation. Where their faithful feet tread, there especially

the Lord will send the blessing of water and the green of new life
(v.6). Sometimes, indeed, the first rains already begin, forming
pools on the rock-hard earth; but in other years, they have still to be
waited for. In any event, the power sent out from God helps the
weary feet ever more and more; 'from strength to strength' the
pilgrims go, until they come to see God's glory in Zion.

8–9   Prayer for the king is introduced with special earnestness.
Brief as this petition is, it may well be the heart of the psalm. The
Lord's Anointed is king and 'shield', titles also of the Lord (vv.3,
11); the point is that he mediates the royal work and protection of
God. The earnest desire of the pilgrims is that their Davidic ruler
should remain in the favour of the Lord, and so pass on the blessing
to all the society.

10–12   Words appreciating the grace of God in temple and life
now resume the opening praises – God will surely hear those who so
trust and rejoice in him. Though the pilgrim's stay in the holy place
is all too short, it is valued above long residence elsewhere. The
Lord is praised as the light of life and the royal defender, the giver
of grace and glory, and also as one who will not withhold 'good'
from a people whole in loyalty. This 'good' may allude especially to
rain and the health of a new year of growth.

The psalm's prayer for the Lord's Anointed is set in a context of
praise – thankfulness for all God gives in the place and time of
worship. The journey which the pilgrims have made is beautifully
reflected. At the outset, when the road leading up to the holy place
was still but a hope in their hearts, strength came to them from God.
In mid-course, treading on the parched land, their faithful steps
were preparing the blessings of water and new life. Arriving, their
soul found its home with the contentment of the swallow that nests
in the holy precincts.

   The picturesque praise still speaks of the beauty and joy that are
found in the time and place where communion is given. The
pilgrim's journey is still a parable of the way to God: the first
aspiration, already nurtured by his grace; the long, hard way where
the fruits of faithfulness will only be seen in his good time; the

coming at last into his courts as to our true home, to be made new in the light of his face. The prayer of verses 8–9 has been taken up by the church to offer Christ's work, asking that the Father will behold his Son in us, and be gracious to us for his sake.

O Lord of Hosts, by your might may the hope of travelling to you be born in our heart; bless our steps through the dry places, that fruit may in time be gathered there for you; and may our soul at last take wing to your holy dwelling, where we shall see you face to face.

Psalm 85

The Kiss of Peace

1 Lord, you once showed favour to your land,
   and restored the life of Jacob.
2 You forgave the offence of your people,
   and covered all their sin.   [Pause]
3 You took away all your indignation,
   and turned back from the heat of your wrath.
4 Restore us again, O God of our salvation,
   and let your anger cease from us.
5 Will you for ever be angry with us,
   will you stretch out your wrath for evermore?
6 Will you not turn again and revive us,
   that your people may rejoice in you?
7 Show us your faithful love, O Lord,
   and give us your salvation.
8 I will hear what the Lord God speaks:
      truly he speaks peace
   for his people, the folk of his covenant –
      only let them not turn back to folly.
9 Even now his salvation is near to those who fear him,
   that glory may dwell in our land.
10 Love and truth have met together;
    right and peace have kissed each other.
11 Truth springs up from the earth,
    and right looks down from heaven.
12 The Lord shall indeed give blessing,
    and our land shall give her produce.
13 Right goes on before him,
    and prepares the way for his steps.

An intercession for God to restore the life of his people (vv. 4–7) is grounded on past experience of his grace (vv. 1–3) and answered by a divine message of assurance (vv. 8–13).

1–3   The supplication opens with reference to former experience of the Lord's favour, transforming grace, atonement, forgiveness and removal of wrath – an experience needed again. The expression in verse 1b gathers all such work of grace into one phrase: God 'turns the great turning' or 'restores with a great restoration' – he restores his people to wonderful life. There is no indication of the occasion of the renewal, which indeed characterized many times of grace.

4–7   Restoration as known in the past is prayed for now. The people have long lain under the shadow of affliction, and earnestly seek that wonder of salvation and faithful love which will restore them again to true life.

8   The singer here, in prophetic manner, introduces the Lord's response to the foregoing petition. After listening for the divine message, he is able to sum it up as 'peace', *shalom*, comprising all the blessings of the covenant, including harmony, health and increase in field, flocks and family. A cautionary note is sounded in the last clause of the verse: to have such *shalom*, they must not return to folly, a foolish self-sufficiency, insensitive to the Lord's will.

9–14   The response of God is not quoted directly, but his good purpose is reported. The faithfulness and grace of his character and actions are seen by the visionary singer as angelic forms, co-operating and hurrying forward to dispense his blessings. These 'angels' are seen in pairs that work in harmony. 'Salvation' and 'glory', representing the saving power and presence of the Lord, are near; they will dwell in the land, centred in the temple. 'Faithful love' and 'truth', representing God's constant and enduring commitment, have come together in close embrace. 'Right' and 'peace', right order in creation and the consequent health and plenty, kiss in loving alliance. As in a vision, the singer sees 'truth' springing up in the green shoots from the happy earth, and 'right' leaning out from heaven to look down benevolently, as will be apparent in the good work of rain and sun. So the Lord will give 'good', the blessing of rain especially, and earth will respond with all her produce. The Lord himself is seen to advance, as sacred processions used to signify, touching the fields with living grace, entering his sanctuary to renew his good rule; and 'right', the angel of cosmic order and harmony, is the herald who prepares his way and signifies his good purpose.

The people are suffering severe deprivation. But can it be that, dark as the scene is, the light is not far away? As the singer waits upon God, conviction is given that the turn to good is near at hand. Angelic powers, reflecting God's heart, are already at work to heal and reconcile, to bless and make fruitful. The Saviour himself is hastening to his people, and they and the good earth will soon be bright with his glory.

The psalm reflects a sense of the connectedness of the spirit and the earth; the world of prayer and faith is also the world of nature. Love and faithfulness, right and goodness are ultimately the divine powers emanating from the Creator which make the order of life. The modern age has moved far from this ancient wisdom, but in our deepest reflections we begin to glimpse again that cosmic unity of spirit and earth, of right and health. So we come to know that life is the blessing of the Creator, and nothing else.

O God, who through your Word sent pardon and peace to restore your creation, cause your people to see afresh your love and be revived by your salvation; and so may we rejoice in the knowledge that you are redeeming all things in your faithfulness.

The Rebirth of the Nations in Love

1 *On the holy mountains is the city he founded;*
2 *the Lord loves even the gates of Zion*
  above all the dwellings of Jacob.
3 *Weighty things are spoken*
  for you, O city of God: [Pause]
4 *I enrol Egypt and Babylon as those who know me;*
  Philistia and Tyre with Ethiopia, each as born there.
5 *Yes, of Zion it shall be said, Each one was born in her,*
  whom the Most High has established.
6 *The Lord shall record, as he writes up the peoples,*
  each one as born there.   [Pause]
7 *And as they dance they shall sing,*
  All my fresh springs are in you.

This song presents Zion as the Lord's dwelling, destined to be the mother-city of all peoples. It may have originated in the part of the autumn festival when thought centred on the temple as purified and reconsecrated, glorious with the new presence of God. An introduction declares the Lord's love for Zion and announces a momentous oracle. God's pronouncement follows in direct speech (v. 4), and is then developed by the prophetic singer. The weighty and visionary content of this psalm is expressed abruptly, especially in verses 1 and 7 – perhaps a prophetic style, shafts of meaning emerging from mysterious depths

1–3 It is a transfigured city that is described, Zion according to her meaning in God's purpose. That he himself founded her, and on the mountains that reach into heaven and bear the very traffic of heaven – all this is to say that she is one with the heavenly sanctuary. She is the place on earth where heaven is disclosed and the Lord of all makes himself known. The founding is itself full of meaning:

here is a bulwark for life and goodness against the vengeful tides of chaos. For this Zion, that also personifies all his worshippers, the Lord has the utmost love and devotion; her very gates are dearer to him that all other 'dwellings' (or perhaps 'shrines') of his people 'Jacob'. And now for this Zion an oracle is to be pronounced – a word and vision from the Lord, heavy with rich significance for her destiny. The prophetic singer addresses her directly as 'city of God' or 'divine city'.

4–7   The inspired message begins with God's own words and continues from verse 5 as the singer's exposition, giving the fuller picture of the visionary scene. The Lord is seen recording the names of those who know him, and it is whole peoples that he is inscribing in this book of life. He writes them down, moreover, as having been born in Zion. But it is, we might say, a new birth, a wonderful transformation, for these had worshipped other gods and were sometimes enemies of Israel. In particular, Egypt here is denoted as 'Rahab', the name of the hostile chaos-monster; but this oppressor of the Exodus is now forgiven. God 'Most High', the Creator and supreme ruler of all, has established his city as embracing a fellowship of all peoples. And the singer concludes by picturing them united in festal worship, dancing with joy in the Lord and singing of the fountains of life that they have found in Zion ('you', a feminine form).

The psalm shows how the worshippers at the temple in Jerusalem might see through to an immense meaning. Because they encountered there the Most High, maker of all peoples, they saw in Zion a summit carrying them into heaven. Around this throne of the Creator all peoples must gather; his pleasure must be in the songs and dances of all. With a visionary leap beyond all historical divisions and enmities, the psalmist sees the Lord enrolling all the peoples as natives of Zion. How this could come about is not explained; only that it has been 'spoken', created beforehand by the divine word.

The little poem lived on when Jerusalem was cruelly destroyed, and is still sung in a world where murderous deeds between ethnic groups are common. Seeing beyond such hatreds, it prefigures a spiritual city where all nations will be born again as fellow citizens, a temple where they will meet with God in his love, a heavenly garden where together they will drink of the fountain of life. Something of this wonder, the New Testament teaches, is already to be experienced – the citizenship that is in heaven (Philippians 3.20), belonging to a Jerusalem that is above, the mother of many children (Galatians 4.26).

O Lord, the Most High, in love you have founded a place where heaven and earth meet, and by your Word you have prepared a new birth for all nations that they may belong to that place; we beseech you to strengthen us in this vision, prepare our spirits in forgiveness and reconciliation, and so bring to pass the time when all shall rejoice together at the wells of your salvation.

Psalm 88

A Plea from the Land without Memory

1   Lord, God of my salvation,
    I cry day and night towards you.
2   May my prayer come into your presence;
    turn your ear towards my crying.
3   For my soul is full of torments,
    and my life has come to the land of death.
4   I am counted with those gone down into the pit;
    I am like one whose strength has departed.
5   My couch is among the dead,
        with the slain that dwell in the tomb,
    whom you remember no more,
        and they are cut off from the help of your hand.
6   You have set me in the lowest pit,
    in a place of darkness in the mighty deeps.
7   Your anger lies heavy upon me,
    and you have afflicted me with all your waves.   [Pause]
8   You have put my friends far from me,
    and made me to be abhorred by them.
    I am imprisoned and cannot go free;
9   my eyes fail through all my trouble.
    Lord, I call to you daily;
    I stretch out my hands to you.
10 Will you do marvels for the dead,
    will the shades rise up to praise you?
11 Shall your love be told in the tomb,
    your faithfulness in the land of the lost?
12 Will your wonders be known in the darkness,
    your goodness in the land without memory?
13 But as for me, Lord, I cry to you;
    even in the dawn my prayer comes early before you.
14 Why, Lord, do you spurn my soul;
    why do you hide your face from me?

15 I am brought low and my strength ebbs away;
    I bear your terrors and am almost gone.
16 Your wrath sweeps over me;
    your horrors bring me to destruction.
17 All day long they come about me like water;
    they close me in on every side.
18 Lover and friend you have put far from me;
    my best companion is now the darkness.

In this supplication the lack of hopeful statements usual in prayers
of distress gives the psalm an especially tragic character. Much of
the imagery for suffering comes from ancient poetic tradition
depicting Sheol, imagined as the universal tomb or home of the
dead, a place of darkness, silence and utter weakness beneath the
subterranean waters. The psalm may be the expression of prayer in
severe sickness.

1–2 The opening plea for a hearing is especially significant in the
context of this sombre psalm. The first word is 'Yahweh' ('Lord'),
the name God gave specifically for 'invocation', for calling down the
saviour into the encircling darkness (Exodus 3.15). The name of
God so used encapsulates an immense tradition of faith and
experience, and at once sets the suffering and the cry to heaven in
the context of a relationship, a mutual knowledge which should
prove stronger than all affliction. The next phrase fills out the name
itself: 'O God of my salvation', that is, 'God my saviour'. The prayer
to this saviour rises night and day, a cry which strives to rise from
the depths to reach his holy throne. This is the nature of all that will
follow. Utterly tragic as it seems, it is all directed to him who alone
can save. Underlying all is a hidden but massive foundation of faith
and hope.

3–9a The plight of the sufferer is now depicted to move the
divine compassion. The soul is sated with harms or injuries, and the
sufferer can therefore be depicted as having already made the
descent into the land of the dead. He is like one of the shades,

finally at rest in this universal tomb. An ancient instinct was that Sheol was an 'unclean' place, and so cut off from God, a place then without the communion of praise. The idea is not consistently maintained; in some texts we hear of the Lord's power to break into that farthest region. Nevertheless, our psalmist's thought is how near he is to being finally lost. He feels to be in the remotest part of Sheol, or again, to be battered by the deadly waves in the jaws of Sheol. Friends keep far off, avoiding the contagion of misfortune. The sufferer feels shut in by walls of misfortune and unable to find a way out.

9b–12   The prayer takes a fresh beginning, invoking again the saviour by name. The pleading questions assume a negative answer; once finally consigned to Sheol, the dead see no wonders of salvation and have no occasion or cult in which to raise thanksgiving and testimony, for all there – such was the ancient belief – lay in the silence of oblivion. The questions take the place of the promise, common in other supplications, to give thanks and praise when deliverance comes. To match the extremity of the situation, the psalmist confines himself to showing the terrible danger that he may soon be beyond the possibility of salvation and consequent praise.

13–18   The question and laments express the belief that it is with the Lord alone that the sufferer wrestles, for it is his will and action that cause the affliction. The vital thought is therefore that God is the one who can change the situation. But the one he cherished he appears now to reject, hiding his face of love. Emissaries of his wrath hem the sufferer in. God has caused all friends to flee away, and the one that can be relied on to stay is the deadly shadow of Sheol.

The psalm gives a voice to all who are in the depths of suffering, almost at the end of their strength. It leads them to direct their supplication again and again to the Lord, the only Saviour. It is a voice also for those who, in loving sympathy, would pray on behalf of any in such extremity.

But further, the poetical nature of the psalm has long encouraged imaginative applications. It became the voice of a whole people in captivity, and then again the ever-renewed prayer of the Christ who suffers in the darkness for the healing of the many. In these many meanings, its plaintive tones have risen from the great deeps of suffering and pleaded early at the gates of heaven. Such prayer that invokes the holy name of the saviour God, so the psalmist believed, does not rise up in vain.

Lord, God of our salvation, hear the cry of those who are full of torments and imprisoned by terrors; have pity on those who have fallen into the land without memory and are cut off from lovers and friends; and by the passion of your Son Jesus, in the mystery of your eternal purpose, raise them up into the light of your face where all is made well.

Psalm 90

Harvesting a Heart of Wisdom

1   Lord, you have been our refuge
    from one generation to another.
2   Before the mountains were born,
        or earth and world brought forth,
    from everlasting and for ever you are God.
3   You turn man back to dust
    and say, Return, O children of earth.
4   A thousand years in your eyes are but as yesterday;
    they pass like a watch of the night.
5   You carry them away, as though but a dream.
    In the morning they grow up like the grass,
6   early they blossom and flourish;
    by evening they droop and wither away.
7   Truly, we are consumed by your anger,
    and troubled by your wrath.
8   You have set our misdeeds before you,
    our secret faults in the light of your face.
9   All our days decline in your wrath;
    we spend our days like a sigh.
10 The days of our years may reach seventy years,
    or eighty if strength is great.
    Yet their span is but toil and trouble;
    quickly it passes, and we fly away.
11 Who knows the power of your anger,
    and your wrath, as you should be feared?
12 So teach us to number our days,
    that we may harvest a heart of wisdom.
13 Turn us again, Lord; O how long?
    Have pity on your servants.
14 Satisfy us in the morning with your faithful love,
    that we may sing and rejoice though all our days.
15 Gladden us for all the days you have afflicted us,
    and for the years we have seen adversity.

16 *Let your work be revealed to your servants,*
   and your glory be over their children.
17 *May the beauty of the Lord our God be upon us;*
   and prosper the work of our hands for us,
      O prosper the work of our hands.

This is a supplication of the community in some long affliction. It seems to be a long period of economic hardship when the labour of the hands goes to waste (v.17). The hope for help 'in the morning' (v.14) is possibly an indication that the worshippers are keeping a night vigil and looking for an answer at the break of day.

1–6   The psalm first calls on 'Adonay' ('Lord'), the sovereign of all. And the first thought is then of the help with which he has sustained his people in time past. Shall it not be so again? In verses 2–6 the consideration put before God is the brevity of human life – how fleeting against the eternity of God! An ancient conception of creation is reflected in verse 2 – earth as giving birth to mountains and living things. Made from the earth, humans return to it as fine dust (Genesis 3.19). What slight duration this must seem to the Lord for whom a thousand years are but a flicker! People are transient as Palestine's green things – fresh in the cool of the morning, but finished by a day of burning wind or sun. Should such a brief life be spent in suffering? So the psalmist would stir the pity of God.

7–12   The present distress of the worshippers is now laid before God. They interpret the long hardship as sent by God in anger at their sins. So the days pass away without apparent fruit or value – like a mere breath. At verse 10 the thought turns again to the general human lot, its transience being a consideration to move God's compassion. And who can fear God with the fear due to him? This grave thought prompts a prayer in verse 12 that God will teach his people so to realize their transience that they may 'bring in' (as harvest) a heart of wisdom.

13–17 The main prayer now unfolds in the form of several petitions. May the Lord return to his loving dealings with his people. How long until he have pity? Verse 14 may refer to the hope of a sign or word given as morning breaks, a signal of a new time of salvation. May there be joy enough to make up for the days of affliction. May the Lord's saving work appear, the light and beauty of his face. So the work in fields and home will be founded in his grace, proving fruitful once more.

Adverse conditions for cultivation and produce could quickly devastate such a society. Many troubled years lie behind this psalm. O that the Lord would again show the beauty of his face; O that his light would shine upon the toiling hands and establish all their work in fruitfulness! In pity may he regard his people, so fleeting in their stay among the living, and grant them days of joy. And with his compassion, there is also the commitment he made as Creator and revealed Lord. May the morning be a daybreak of this faithful love.

The psalm is set within the boundaries of a faith which humbly accepted only life on earth as God's allotment to the human race. If we truly recollect our mortality, it says, we may harvest a wise heart that finds peace within the boundaries God has made. When a greater hope became general, this old wisdom still had its value. The hope in God's compassion and steadfast love, a hope sustained in profound realism and humility, was a precious heritage for ever.

Eternal Lord, help us to take to heart the brevity of our time on earth, and so gain wisdom to live here in reverence and humility; prosper the work of our hands, and satisfy us with the morning light of your faithful love, through your son Jesus, who is the fulfilment of all our hope.

∾ Psalm 93 ∾

Proclaiming the Kingdom

1 *The Lord is King! He has robed himself in majesty;*
he has robed himself, yes, girded himself with glory.
So the world is established;
it shall not be overthrown.
2 *Your throne was established of old;*
you are from everlasting.
3 *The rivers lifted, O Lord, then lifted the rivers their voice;*
the rivers lifted up their din.
4 *More than the thunders of the mighty waters,*
   than the glorious breakers of the sea,
more glorious was the Lord on high.
5 *Your commands are very sure;*
holiness adorns your house, O Lord, for evermore.

An ancient psalm from the heart of the autumn festival, it proclaims
the new reign of the Lord, with the establishment of the world, as
the consequence of his mastering the chaos represented by the
water-powers. In the mysteries of worship, where the long line of
time is dissolved or transcended, the first founding of the world is
present again, and the Lord's reign begins. The worshippers find
assurance that creation, growth, life and blessing will be known in
the coming year, as the glory of the Lord, the King, now shines from
his newly sanctified temple.

1–2 The singer proclaims the meaning of the dramatic moment in
worship. In movements with processions and acclamations, the
supremacy of the Lord as Creator and ruler is shown, and the
psalmist brings out this essential meaning in terse, ancient phrases.
Unworthy contenders for the throne have been routed. Proclamation is thus made that the Lord begins his reign, taking the throne
in the robes of his unique majesty, glory and power. The new reign

means that an order of joyful life is established; the earth has been made firm in all the conditions for life. The singer addresses praise to the Creator as the One whose sovereignty was destined from eternity, from the unimaginable and ultimate beginning.

3–4 Continuing his tribute of praise, the singer recalls the Lord's victory over the chaos-waters, the victory seen in poetic traditions as crucial to creation, the waters being made to serve the economy of life. The style here is like that of very ancient poetry from Syria that personifies the water-powers with titles. We might render more literally: 'More than the thunders of their Majesties the Waters, of their Lordships the Breakers of the Sea, more lordly on high was Yahweh.' The effect is ironic. These would-be kings rose up to do battle, proud waters that reared and dashed with thunderous voices. But the outcome proved that it was to the Lord, high above them, that the true majesty belonged.

5 The singer's praise moves on to the consequences of the creation-victory – the joyful present and its prospect. The 'commands' of the Lord are especially his mighty words that constituted and ordered the living world and ever sustain it; they are 'sure' in that they are effective and also a source of confidence, trust and gladness. The 'house' of the Lord is his heavenly abode, but also its earthly manifestation in Zion; the rites of new year will have included the cleansing of the temple for his re-entry. Its beauty of holiness is its reflection of the glory of the Lord in his new presence as victorious king; it is itself a sign of his established reign.

In the drama of festal worship, the founding acts of God could be celebrated year by year as present and new; here was an experience that filled the present with joy and cast beams of light into the days to come. When read outside this original context, the psalm might seem to depict a scene at the end of the present age, a world beyond evil and suffering, where only the good reign of God, finally triumphant, is known. But as a song in worship, the psalm is able to lead into a present experience of the Lord's triumph and perfect reign. Those led to share its vision are replenished now in hope and granted a joy which the upsurgings of evil cannot kill; they live already in the certainty of the kingdom.

Open, O Lord, the eyes of our heart, that we may already see you as victor over all evil, the eternal King of Peace; may we love your commands, and adore you in the beauty of your house for ever.

Joy, Awe and Listening in the Presence of the Lord

1   *Come, let us sing out to the Lord;*
      let us acclaim the rock of our salvation.
2   *Let us come before his face with thanksgiving;*
      let us acclaim him with psalms of praise.
3   *For the Lord is the great God,*
      the great King over all the gods.
4   *In his hand are the depths of the earth,*
      and his also are the peaks of the mountains.
5   *The sea is his, for he made it;*
      the dry land also, which his hands formed.
6   *Come, let us worship and bow down;*
      let us kneel before the Lord our maker.
7   *For he is our God,*
      and we are the people of his pasture,
        the flock tended by his hand.
      O that today you would hear his voice:
8   *Do not harden your hearts as at Meribah,*
      on that day at Massah in the wilderness,
9   *when your fathers tried me;*
      they tested me, though they had seen my work.
10   *Through forty years I was sickened by that generation,*
      till I said, These are a wayward people,
        for they do not know my ways.
11   *So then I vowed in my anger:*
      They shall not enter into my rest.

Another psalm probably from the autumnal new year celebrations. The great procession is entering the temple courts, and the manifestation of the 'face' of the Lord in his royal glory is proclaimed. This holy effulgence is acclaimed with joy, but then follows an awesome speech. The ascended Lord is now to address his people through his minister. Here we see a kind of prophesying long rooted in worship.

1–5   With joyful songs and thanksgiving, God is hailed by the worshippers as rock of their salvation. They are 'coming' or 'entering' before his face; a great procession enters the temple courts, conscious of coming into his holy presence. Such acclamation is fitting because he is revealed as high above all the powers of heaven, owner and Lord of earth and sea.

6–7ab   Advancing a little, the procession must now bow down before the Holy One, acknowledging the Creator as *'our* Maker', *'our* God'. For them especially he is Covenant-Lord and Shepherd.

7c   A prophetic voice, perhaps that of the previous singer adopting the role of God's spokesperson, utters an introduction to the message; we may compare the introductory words in 85.8a. Hidden in the 'O that today you would hear' is the world of blessing which could be theirs, but the word now carries warning. It is for all to hear and respond and this very day to enter into the true life with him, their Lord and Saviour.

8–11   Now comes the oracle, the direct speech of the Lord. He calls on the people not to harden their hearts; not to close their hearts away from trust, patience and love, yielding readily to grumbling and disbelief. The 'hardened' heart is one without living relationship to the Lord, no longer hearing, attentive, trusting, centred on his will, but rather awake only to immediate desires and impulses. The bulk of the oracle, as a warning, recalls the story of the wilderness generation which, having hardened its hearts in particular incidents and also throughout the forty years, did not live to enter the promised land, God's 'rest', his blessed abode. (Tradition told of various episodes at Meribah and Massah, names meaning Dispute and Trial.) The sudden ending of the psalm at this point gives the warning great solemnity; a whole generation can lose its living relationship to the Lord and so miss the goal of its life-journey – what then of the present generation?

The psalm shows the test of true praise as the readiness to hear. Joy in worship is here complementary to willingness to hear God's voice, even in stern warning. The rich significance of this psalm is shown not only by its use in the New Testament (Hebrews 3.7–4.13), but also by its daily use in the church down the centuries. Morning by morning it has invited God's people to pass through the sacred gates and kneel before the face of the Lord; to rejoice in acclaiming him our rock, our shepherd, our Creator, in whose hand rests the world, even to its most mysterious depths and heights. And morning by morning also it has placed great importance on this present moment of encounter, the 'today' in which the Lord of the church binds his people to himself and sets before them his way, the way of the responsive heart. His 'rest', his beautiful country, lies before them, but every day the psalm has voiced his earnest warning against the hard heart that would keep them from it.

O Lord our maker, send, we pray, your Holy Spirit into our hearts, that they may not be hardened towards you or our fellow creatures; and bring us every day to worship before your face and hear your voice, that we may enter into your rest, and know you as the rock of our salvation.

Psalm 98

The Marvellous Circle Won by God's Holy Arm

1 Sing to the Lord a new song,
   for he has done marvellous things.
   His own right hand and his holy arm
   have wrought salvation for him.
2 The Lord has made known his salvation;
   before the eyes of the nations he has shown his justice.
3 He has remembered his love and faithfulness
     to the house of Israel;
   all the ends of the earth have seen the salvation of our God.
4 Acclaim the Lord, all the earth;
   break into singing and make music.
5 Make melody to the Lord with the lyre,
   with the lyre and the voice of song.
6 With trumpets and the voice of the horn,
   sound praise before the Lord the King.
7 Let the sea thunder and all that fills it,
   the round earth and all its creatures.
8 Let the rivers clap their hands,
   the mountains also join the praise,
9 before the Lord who has come to rule the earth;
   he will rule the world with right,
     and the peoples with his justice.

This will be from the high moment in the autumn festival. In a great sacrament of renewal, the Lord has come to his people as Creator-King. The worshippers see about him an ideal world, which we can interpret as both a hope for the new year and an earnest of the ultimate new creation.

1–3 The call for a 'new song' reflects the sense of a new order, the new reign of the Lord. The ancient marvels fundamental to the society embrace both the whole earth (as creation, establishment of living order) and 'the house of Israel' (as the grace of the Exodus and Covenant 'remembered', made new). Such marvellous work, now renewed, is seen as having preceded the Lord's ascent to his temple and his glorious presence proclaimed before his worshippers.

4–9   The acclamations are for the victorious King, ascended to the sound of trumpets and ram's horn (47.5), hailed also in psalmody with voice and music. To this glorious Creator must also be given praise from the great elements and from all living beings, thanksgiving for the victory over chaos and for the reign that creates and sustains the order of life. In the chorus of praise the great oceans contribute their thunder, the bounding streams clap their hands, and the mountains sing to the rhythm; all creatures in their own way offer up the movements and sound of thankful joy to the giver of their life. The Lord is revealed in his temple (v.9), victorious and supreme, faithful and bearing salvation, at the outset of a reign of right and of all that is good.

The church appointed this thrilling psalm for daily uses and for several festivals, including Christmas Day. It has also been used in evening prayer as an alternative to the Magnificat, bridging the Old and New Testament readings. In such usage it calls upon all the world of creation to sing, play and dance to the Lord who in Christ has 'gotten the victory', fulfilling the promise given to the house of Israel, establishing the good kingdom over all that he has made.

Very precious is the psalm's vision of worship as far transcending the praises of one nation and indeed of all nations. Reconciled to each other as worshippers must be, bound in a new mutual respect and love, these myriad creatures of God find joy in being wholly centred on their Creator. The scene is as ultimate as ultimate can be, involving a drastic revolution in our ways; but it is nothing if not a present reality, more real than what passes for reality, and the true worshippers of God, those who know his salvation, must enter it now.

✤

We thank you, Lord, for poets and artists who lead us into love of your creatures, and for the psalms which reveal the fulfilment of such love in your kingdom; help us to respond without delay and enter the circle of praise, that with earth and oceans, rivers and mountains and all that lives in them, we may give thanks for your marvellous salvation, through Christ the Word by whom all things were made.

Psalm 103

The Soul that Finds God's World

1   Bless the Lord, O my soul,
    and all that is within me, bless his holy name.
2   Bless the Lord, O my soul,
    and do not forget all he does for you,
3   forgiving all your wrongdoing,
    healing all your sicknesses,
4   redeeming your life from death's hold,
    encircling you with faithful love and compassion,
5   satisfying you daily with good things,
    so that your youth is renewed as an eagle's.
6   The Lord does deeds of salvation
    and justice for all the oppressed.
7   He made known his ways to Moses,
    his deeds to the children of Israel.
8   Compassionate and gracious is the Lord,
    patient and plenteous in faithful love.
9   He will not always be contending,
    nor for ever be displeased.
10 He has not dealt with us according to our sins,
    nor rewarded us according to our offences.
11 For as the heavens are high above the earth,
    so great is his love over those who fear him.
12 As far as the east is from the west,
    so far has he removed our sins from us.
13 As a father has pity on his children,
    so the Lord has pity on those who fear him.
14 For well he knows how we are formed;
    he is mindful that we are but clay.
15 Man's days are but as grass;
    he flowers like the flower of the field;
16 when a wind passes over him he is gone,
    and his very place will know him no more.

17 But the faithful love of the Lord is from of old and for ever
        upon those who fear him,
     and his goodness upon children's children,
18 for those who keep his covenant,
     and remember his commandments and do them.
19 The Lord has established his throne in heaven,
     and his kingship rules over all.
20 Bless the Lord, you his angels,
     you mighty ones who do his bidding
        and obey the voice of his word.
21 Bless the Lord, all his hosts,
     you servants who do his pleasure.
22 Bless the Lord, all that he has made,
        in all places of his dominion;
     bless the Lord, O you my soul.

We may imagine this beautiful psalm as intended for the assembly
at the autumn festival when the ceremonies have signified atonement
and forgiveness, renewal of the springs of life, and the proclamation
of the Lord's kingship over all. The 'individual' form of the opening
would then be a variation of the usual calls to praise, the singer
giving the lead and example for every one present to engage their
whole heart.

1–5 The summons to praise the Lord takes the form of self-
exhortation. Of several words that might have been chosen for
praise, 'bless' is our poet's choice, used moreover three times here
and four times at the end. It is the word for praise most warm with
gratitude. By the 'soul' and 'all my inward parts' is meant the very
core of one's being, with all the powers of heart and mind; by God's
'name' is meant the form of his making himself known, giving
himself in power and grace. Alas, when relief is given, the heart
easily comes to take it for granted; so 'do not forget' urges the
singer, 'do not forget all his deeds.' These acts of grace are then
depicted in general terms. He, and none but he, is the one who
forgives, heals from sickness, wins back from the abyss, encircles

with tenderness and faithfulness, constantly nourishes with good things. The comparison with the eagle (or griffon-vulture), similar to that in Isaiah 40.31, may refer to the great bird's renewal of feathers after moulting, or simply to its amazing flight as it soars effortlessly to great heights on currents of warm air.

6–18 The reasons for thankful praise are now continued in the more usual style, cataloguing the Lord's saving deeds on behalf of the oppressed, and so for the enslaved people of Israel. Ever since their deliverance he has been proclaimed as the compassionate and faithful one, slow to anger (Exodus 34.5f). The divine forgiveness is especially dwelt upon. His is a love which will not easily give up; its persistence is compared to that of a father for his children. Moreover, the Lord is eager to utterly remove the sins, with all their guilt and entail. He is mindful of human frailty and transience, and through his faithful love he gives an enduring meaning to human life, expressed here as the continuity of life running through the generations.

19–22 The skilful psalmist now moves into his widest perspective. He echoes the great proclamation of the festival that the Lord has established his throne and kingdom, his reign breaking with new light and glory over all the world. The great circle summoned to bless him now extends to his servants in the heavenly sphere and indeed to all he has made, all his creatures. All the 'places of his dominion' can be understood as comprehending the wondrous places remote from our experience, but ever open to the presence of God the King. And the round of praise returns at last to its starting point, the overflowing gratitude of the singer's inmost being.

Here is a small key that opens to mighty spaces. From the warm response of a single soul, the way leads to the fellowship of the people that fear God, to all who have known deliverance from oppression, on to the ministers of the heavens, and so to all created beings. In the thankful sincerity of the one soul lies the capacity to love God as he is and the world as it will be. The thankfulness centres in the experience of forgiveness; it is the knowledge of God as the awesome One who upholds all that is just and good, and yet is full of pity and mercy, patient, and wonderful in his tenacious and abundant love. His forgiveness delivers from the dark abyss, and gives new life as the redeemed soul rises on the breath of his Spirit. Against the fleeting nature of life is set the enduring love of God. Belief will grow that, blessing God, the soul in turn is blessed with a place in the heart of God that will never be lost.

Father, grant us the heart to bless you with such sincerity that we are drawn ever deeper into your forgiving love and your renewing grace; may we rejoice to keep your covenant and do your commandments, as you have removed our sins far from us by your mercy in Jesus Christ.

A Sweet Song of Adoration for the Creator

1   *Bless the Lord, O my soul.*
O Lord my God, you appear in glory.
You have put on majesty and splendour,

2   *and wrapped yourself in light as in a garment.*
You spread out the heavens like a curtain,

3   *and in their waters laid the beams of your high dwelling.*
You make the clouds your chariot,
and ride on the wings of the wind.

4   *You make the winds your messengers,*
and fire and flame your servants.

5   *You founded the earth upon its pillars,*
that it should never be overthrown.

6   *The deep covered it like a garment,*
the waters stood high above the hills.

7   *At your rebuke they fled;*
at the voice of your thunder they hastened away.

8   *They went up the mountains, they went down the valleys,*
to the place which you appointed for them.

9   *You set them their bounds that they should not pass,*
nor turn again to cover the earth.

10   *You send the springs into the brooks*
to run among the hills.

11   *They give drink to every creature of the field;*
the wild asses quench their thirst.

12   *By the brooks dwell the birds of the heavens,*
and give voice among the branches.

13   *From your high dwelling you water the hills,*
and the earth is replenished through all your work.

14   *You make grass to grow for the cattle,*
and crops for the labour of the people,
to bring forth food from the earth,

15   and wine that gladdens their heart,
       oil that makes their faces to shine,
       and bread to sustain their heart.
16   The trees of the Lord are well nourished,
       the cedars of Lebanon which he himself has planted,
17   where the birds make their nests,
       while the stork has her house in the fir trees.
18   The wild goats have the highest mountains;
       the rock badgers find refuge in the cliffs.
19   You made the moon to mark the seasons,
       and the sun that knows his time to set.
20   You made darkness that night may fall,
       when all the beasts of the forest creep forth.
21   The lions roar for their portion,
       and seek their food from God.
22   The sun rises and they are gone,
       to lie down to rest in their dens.
23   Then the people go out to their work
       and to labour until the evening.
24   How many are your works, O Lord,
          and all of them done with wisdom!
       The earth is filled with your creatures.
25   Yonder is the sea, great and wide,
       and there move creatures beyond number,
          both small and great.
26   There go the ships, and there is Leviathan,
       whom you formed to play in the waves.
27   These all look to you,
       to give them their food at the proper time.
28   When you give it them they gather it;
       you open your hand and they are filled with good.
29   When you hide your face they are troubled;
       when you take away their breath,
          they die and return to their clay.
30   When you send out your Spirit they are created,
       and you renew the face of the ground.
31   May the glory of the Lord be for evermore,
       and the Lord ever rejoice in his works,

32   *who but looks on the earth and it trembles,*
      or touches the mountains and they smoke.
33   *I will sing to the Lord as long as I live;*
      I will make music to my God while I have my being.
34   *So shall my song be sweet to him,*
      while I rejoice in the Lord.
35   *Let sinners be taken from the earth, and the wicked be no more;*
      bless the Lord, O you my soul.

There are striking similarities here with Egyptian materials from the second millennium BCE, especially the beautiful hymn of the pharaoh Akhenaton. While remaining entirely true to the Israelite faith and traditions of creation, our psalmist seems to have inherited Egyptian influence, probably passed down from the pre-Israelite poets of Jerusalem who had lived under Egyptian empire. One may wonder if our psalm, like the Egyptian hymn, was meant as a king's personal act of praise. It would still have significance for the people and the world, not least in defending them with prayer from the evil ones (v.35).

1–4   The singer first praises the present manifestation of the Lord, a revelation of his greatness. God appears in royal splendour, the victorious Creator. His work is recalled in several features – the spreading of the heavens like an arch or canopy above the earth, undergirding the heavenly ocean; the founding of the heavenly palace or temple in these waters; the riding of God across the heavens on clouds and the wings of the wind, attended by angelic servants of storm and lightning.

5–9   Tribute to the Creator continues with reference to the firm foundation of the earth upon its bases, the bottoms of the great mountains. Then reference is made to the vital work of mastering and organizing the waters. The great deep that covered the earth was put to flight by the thunder-roar of the warrior-Creator, then divided, with part driven up to become the heavenly ocean, and part sent down through the clefts to form the subterranean waters.

10–18   The tribute of praise now passes on to the present and continuing work of the Creator. From his kingship over the waters he is able to dispense the gifts of life. Out in the wilderness and remote mountains, where man's control is not known, the Creator's care of his creatures is a special source of wonder. He makes the brooks to provide for the onager or wild ass and other animals. The flood-beds produce belts of trees and shrubs along the banks, where the birds nest happily and 'give voice' (in many kinds of utterance). From the waters imagined as stored in the roof chambers of his heavenly palace, the Lord pours down rains to saturate the earth, producing grass for the animals and crops to be turned by human labour into bread, wine and oil. Especially wonderful are the giant trees which only the Lord could have planted and tended, the cedars of Mount Lebanon. Here again is provision for birds, though it is in the fir trees that the huge nests, the 'houses', of the stork are prominent. The great craggy mountains are there for the nimbly leaping ibex or wild goats, and also for the rock hyraxes. These latter animals, about the size of a rabbit and with round backs and no visible tail, can tread surely on steep rocky surfaces; they love to sit in groups in the sun, while one is posted to keep guard as a sentry.

19–23   The Lord's care is further seen in the wonders of night and morning. He made the moon to mark the round of months and holy days; he made the sun, so regular to set and leave the world to darkness. In the darkness nocturnal animals have their proper turn, and the roar of lions is their prayer to God for their due portion. Sunrise again is the proper time for the commencement of human labour. So God makes provision for all.

24–26   The psalmist exclaims at the sheer multitude of creatures in earth and sea, and each one created with 'wisdom', the divine quality of understanding and skill. The ships that float and make their way by the winds become part of the wonderful scene of the great open sea, and the sight of large marine creatures leaping and turning in the waves is reflected in the myth of Leviathan, the personification of the chaos-waters as a fearsome sea-monster that the Lord was able to control and make part of his benevolent kingdom (Job 41).

27–30   Wonder extends not only to the creation, but also to the continuing care and sustenance of these myriads. There is not one that does not look to God for food from his hand. The time comes when he lets them be troubled and die, and turn again to the elemental material from which he had formed them. But then comes re-creation and renewal, when God sends forth his Breath or Spirit, from which is derived the living spirit of every creature. So the face of the earth is renewed, and plants and animals live again.

31–35   A blessing-wish is offered for the everlasting splendour and joy of the Creator in all his works, he who is so mighty that a look or a touch from him can bring earthquakes and volcanic eruptions. Perhaps we discern the kingly character of the psalmist not only in the commitment to continual praise through temple music, but also in the prayer against the sinners and wicked of the earth. May those who would defile and ruin the good world of life be removed from it. Here we glimpse the responsibility of our race to guard the treasure of life, not least by strong and continuing prayer.

Readily the soul may wonder at the curtain of heaven, the stores of water on high and below, the animals of the wild that find their places to drink, the birds that weave their nests and sing their countless melodies, the little animals that tread the rock-faces so surely, the seedtime and harvest, the constancies of moon and sun, dark and light, the width of the sea, the play of dolphins, the course of the ships through waves and wind. But for our psalmist, the real wonder is the wisdom and glory of God discerned in all these things. The world indeed is vast and multitudinous in its kinds, but the beginning and end of this meditation is the soul that recognizes and blesses the Lord in it all.

   Notable is the way the poet puts human beings within his list of the creatures that depend on the Lord; they appear humbly alongside their fellow creatures. Time was when the concluding prayer (v.35) might be found jarring within the sweet meditation.

But as human exploitation becomes ever more comprehensive, the prayer against the ruining of earth's order and species is seen as ever more important. Coming at the end of the psalm, it can be read as its climax. The sinners that exploit to ruination are many indeed, and the prayer for the removal of this cruel work from the good kingdom of life must burst from the soul that has loved and wondered at the creatures of God.

O glorious God, creating and caring for all that has being, help us to sing to you through all our life with the sweetness of joyful adoration; deepen our tenderness for all your creatures and take from the hearts of all people the callousness and greed which harm your world.

❧ Psalm 113 ❧

The Lord who Humbles Himself

1   Alleluia.
    Praise, you servants of the Lord,
    O praise the name of the Lord.
2   May the name of the Lord be blessed,
    from now and for evermore.
3   From the rising of the sun to its setting,
    may the name of the Lord be praised.
4   High above all nations is the Lord,
    and his glory is above the heavens.
5   Who is like the Lord our God,
    that has his throne so high,
6   yet humbles himself to behold
    the things of heaven and earth;
7   taking up the poor from the dust,
    lifting the destitute from the ash-heap,
8   making them sit with princes,
    with the princes of his people;
9   giving peace to the barren wife,
    making her a joyful mother of children?
    Alleluia.

This is likely to have been intended for a great occasion of worship, the congregation being addressed as 'servants of the Lord'. The Lord is praised as raising the poor from the utmost degradation and as wonderfully changing the fortune of a barren wife. This is the first of the group of praising psalms (113–118) which came to be known as 'the Hallel' ('hymn of praise'). At family Passovers 113–114 were sung before and 115–118 after the meal, and perhaps therefore at the Last Supper (Matthew 26.30; Mark 14.26).

1–3 The singer's call goes out to the 'servants of the Lord'; probably meaning the whole congregation of his worshippers. Indeed, those gathered at the temple represent the whole world of his creatures. They are to praise and bless his 'name' (specified thrice), the form in which he reaches out to his creatures, making himself known in glory and accessible in grace.

4–9 At first it seems that the praise will consist of tribute to his exaltation above all on earth and in heaven. But the thankful praise unfolds further. The greatest wonder is that this king, who 'shows exalted supremacy' in his throne above all that exists, 'shows lowliness' in taking heed of the suffering of his little ones and acting to save them. This highest of all lords thus comes to the heaps outside the town, where the community's garbage and filth is collected and incinerated; here he finds the outcasts of society scavenging to keep alive, homeless and friendless. He restores them to honoured life, to sit indeed among the noblest. Or again, he takes note of the misery of a barren wife, an especially acute grief in that society; he gives her a highly honoured place in the family group, as she becomes the joyful mother of (literally) 'sons'.

The examples of salvation given in the psalm do not describe things happening with monotonous regularity; though they are indeed characteristic of the Lord, many an outcast has remained at the refuse tips, and many a wife has had to carry her grief to the end. Worshippers, ancient and modern, have always known this. But the examples represent the experience of grace which animates all true praise. When the rational mind could not expect it, when hope itself was running low, the saving power has come and transformed the situation of grief. The later Jewish worshippers, including the disciples of Jesus, would think of the nation that the Lord had saved and would save again, and of the mother-city that would be blessed with many children. But the individual reference of the psalm's examples remains important; that experience of a saving love beyond all expectation is known fully only by the one saved, who then contributes fervently to the world of praise.

A special beauty of the psalm is its sense of the divine humility, the readiness of the highly enthroned one to care for the lowest and loneliest. The New Testament sees this grace embodied in the Lord Jesus, to be reflected in his disciples (Mark 2.15f; John 13.2f; Philippians 2.5f).

We bless your name, O Lord, the name above all names, and we thank you that from your high throne you have seen the wretched and humbled yourself to save them; grant that this mind be in us, that we also humble ourselves, and take our part as obedient servants in your work of salvation.

The Holy One in his People

1   When Israel came out of Egypt,
     the house of Jacob from a people strange in speech,

2   Judah became his sanctuary,
     Israel the heart of his dominion.

3   The sea but looked and fled,
     the Jordan ran back in its course.

4   The mountains skipped like rams,
     the hills like lambs and kids.

5   What ails you, O sea, that you flee away,
     and Jordan that you run back,

6   you mountains that you skip like rams,
     you hills like lambs and kids?

7   Tremble, O earth, at the presence of the Lord,
     at the presence of the God of Jacob,

8   who turns hard rock into a pool of water,
     flint-stone into a springing well.

A psalm so terse and dramatic! Perhaps due to a setting in worship where the old story was vividly relived in ritual and song, the force of the psalm is all for actualization – making the scene present. It moves swiftly from introductory reference to the Exodus to the marvels and consternation in waters and mountains, and then deftly makes these upheavals present, concluding with a call for trembling now at the powerful presence of God. Such celebration of the Exodus would be in place at the Passover, but also in the autumn festival (which dominated in and around the royal period).

1–2   Just one feature of Israel's life in Egypt is mentioned – the language (partly of African character) which seemed so strange. With this one feature, the poet conjures up a place of discomfort, insecurity, hostility, a place which is not home. But at that coming out, that Exodus, there occurred the amazing event which founded the enduring mystery of Israel's significance. This people became the bearer of the divine presence; God was pleased to centre in them his holy power, his royal glory. The parallel statements of verse 2 are best taken as two sides of the same coin; 'Judah' and 'Israel' are the main blocks of the tribal people which together are the bearers of the presence of God. The lack of the naming of God makes no difficulty for the sense in such a well-known story, but the naming, when it comes at last in verse 7, will be all the more striking.

3–4 The flight of the waters is an echo of the creation battle. The consternation of the mountains is a common feature of accounts of God's appearing. With these reactions in nature to the fearful presence of God in his people, the psalmist sweeps on from the Exodus to the crossing of the Jordan (Joshua 3.9–17) and the entry into Canaan; the years of wilderness wanderings, however, will be glimpsed in verse 8.

5–6 Taking up the very words of the preceding description, the psalmist asks the waters and mountains the reason for their consternation. The living personalities of sea, river, mountains and hills (as later also the earth) are brought out even more by his address to them; but his question further makes the transition from an account of ancient events to a present reality. It is the question of one who with amazement witnesses the fleeing waters and leaping hills.

7–8 The singer provides his own answer, implying 'Yes, you do well to be in consternation...'. He calls to the whole earth to tremble before the manifest Master and sovereign Lord (*adon*), owner of all the lands, and Covenant-lord of this people 'Jacob'. In evidence of the power of this God, reference is made only to the wilderness miracle (Exodus 17.6); here the positive aspect of the divine power is seized upon, the creation of the spring of life from the hard and barren rock.

This is a song to bring the listening worshippers into an awesome scene. With the waves of the Reed Sea, the currents of the Jordan, the great mountains and the rolling hills, they too are to tremble in the presence of the King of creation, mighty in his purpose of redemption. The Christian use of the psalm at Easter and in the offices for the dying and the dead have continued the psalmist's work of actualization. The church here recognizes her Lord who has made his sanctuary within his people, leads them through the waters of death, and gives from the hard rock of his sufferings the water of life. The Exodus becomes real also for the individual, who is granted safe passage through death's waters and entrance into the land of divine rest. Down the centuries the psalm has been sung to Tonus Peregrinus, 'the pilgrim's tune', handed down from ancient psalmody; for church and individual it is indeed a good song of pilgrimage – arresting, dramatic, bringing the sense of the living world that responds to its almighty Lord, and revealing this Lord himself, ever present, ever active in redemption.

Make real to us, great Lord, the wonders of your ancient work, that we may know you present still as saviour and guide of your people; so may we also tremble and worship, and drink deep of the springing well of your salvation.

❦ Psalm 121 ❦

The Hills of Hope

1   *I lift up my eyes to the hills;*
     O from where shall my help come?
2   *My help will come from the Lord,*
     the maker of heaven and earth.
3   *He will not let your foot be tripped;*
     he who guards you will not slumber.
4   *See, the guardian of Israel*
     will neither slumber nor sleep.
5   *The Lord himself is your guardian;*
     the Lord at your right hand will be your shade.
6   *By day the sun shall not strike you,*
     nor shall the moon by night.
7   *The Lord will guard you from all evil;*
     he himself will guard your soul.
8   *The Lord will guard your going out and your coming in,*
     from now and for evermore.

A singer in need expresses trust (vv.1–2), and is answered by divine affirmation. From the Creator, the guardian of Israel, protection is promised by day and night and for ever; he will be at this person's right hand, ever vigilant, defending from all harm. The weight of these assurances would be appropriate originally for the king, and reasons and conditions would have been treated in other moments of the worship. Here it is enough that the supplicant has expressed trust.

1–2   The worshipper (the community's head or representative) asks a question in order to give a resounding answer. Looking up to the heights, he asks where his salvation is to come from, and testifies that it will be only from the Lord, the Creator of heaven and earth.

3–8 A singer now addresses the supplicant (with 'you' singular), unfolding assurances of the Lord's protection. It is like an indirect oracle, delivered with the authority of one inspired by God. The Creator is now further entitled 'guardian of Israel', and the verb 'to guard / keep' is used prominently – six times in six verses. Like a good shepherd or city watchman, he will not forsake his vigilance (a contrast may be intended with the nature gods supposed to 'sleep' in summer). At his beloved's right hand, he is 'shade' against the fierce sun; the word suggests the dominion of the heavenly king spread over his servant in closest care. Verse 6b reflects the widely held view that the moon also could strike with various maladies. The 'going out and coming in' means the beginning and finishing of any undertaking, and is especially applied to rulers.

As though from a valley of suffering, a supplicant raises eyes to the hills. Whence shall come the light of salvation? He holds fast to his trust in the Lord; he believes that the angels of faithfulness and comfort will appear in a new dawn, heralding the Lord's own coming. A voice of assurance then sounds; the minister of God promises unceasing protection from all harm, and for ever.

There is a mystery in this divine protection. Again and again it is known in all its wonder and grace. But how often again it seems absent, and the eyes strain up to the hills in vain! The glowing promises seem to come from the royal ideals, and so their fulfilment is to be sought in the royal Messiah. The disciples of Christ must expect to suffer with him, yet guarded by God in deepest mystery, until the secret of that faithful guarding is fully revealed.

Grant, Lord, that when we lift up our eyes to the hills in longing for your help, we may hear and take to our hearts the promise of your unfailing care; may we know that you are guarding us by day and night, as we go out and come in, and that whatever our share in the sufferings of the cross, you are our shade and our saviour, now and for evermore.

Psalm 122

Arriving in Jerusalem

1 I was glad when they said to me,
   We will go to the house of the Lord.
2 And now our feet are standing
   within your gates, O Jerusalem –
3 Jerusalem, you that are built
   as a city bound in fellowship.
4 Here the tribes ascend, the tribes of the Lord,
   as is the law for Israel, to give thanks to the name of the Lord.
5 And here stand thrones for justice,
   the thrones of the house of David.
6 O pray for the peace of Jerusalem;
   may blessing abound on those who love you.
7 Peace be within your walls,
   tranquillity within your palaces.
8 For the sake of my brothers and companions,
   I will pray down peace upon you.
9 For the sake of the house of the Lord our God,
   I will seek good for you.

The setting is probably the autumn festival, the greatest celebration of 'Zion' in the royal period. The psalmist speaks as one who has made the pilgrimage with a party of companions, and is moved to utterance by the thrill of arriving. But rather than being an impromptu, individual song, which had somehow to find its way into the official collections, the psalm more likely is from temple ceremony, the poet making skilful use of the typical pilgrim's experience. Such openness to the genuine feelings of the heart, the very life of the people, is part of the greatness of the Psalms; we might compare the refreshment of formal music through the openness of the great composers to popular melody and dance.

1–2 The singer voices common feelings among the worshippers, beginning with recollection of the excitement at the outset of the pilgrimage. A party was formed to make the journey together (Isaiah 2.3) and now, here they are, standing within the famous gates! Love for the holy city leads the singer to address her as the living Beloved of the Lord. Her name 'Jerusalem' ('foundation of peace') is pronounced three times in the short psalm, preparing for poetic use of its sound and sense in verses 6–8.

3–5 The address to Jerusalem continues. The compact, walled city, nestling in the hills, a beautiful scene from the surrounding heights, is praised as well-suited to the gathered fellowship of pilgrims, representative of all the Lord's tribes. How wonderful she is as the place for all his people, as he has commanded, to acknowledge, bless and praise him in his name, his revelation from his temple! Moreover, she is the centre of justice, that good order given by the Lord through his Anointed and assistant princes, which brings health to society and all the living world.

6–9 The singer now calls upon all the worshippers to pray for this beloved Jerusalem. The remarkable play of sounds in the Hebrew here was probably felt to evoke deep realities of God, all the destiny that was inherent in this place through God's choice and purpose: '*sha'alu shelom yerushalayim, yishleyu ohabayik.*' The pilgrims are to ask peace, *shalom*, for her – tranquillity and all that is good; and the psalmist shows the way with his own example, undertaking to continue praying down peace and well-being upon her. He will seek good for her from God for the sake of all his people, the family of God, for God gives them life through her; also for the sake of the Lord's house, that it may continue in purity and peace as the vessel of the Lord's presence and grace.

From the inexhaustible meaning of the holy city, our psalm draws several great themes. It is the place of the fellowship, the loving unity of the Lord's worshippers. It is the place of the name of the Lord, his presence, his self-giving, where his people find their life renewed as they worship and sing praise. And it is the centre and source of justice, the good order sent by God through his anointed ones, bringing his law to bear on every aspect of life, rescuing, healing, and guiding.

In her deepest meaning, Jerusalem is secure and eternally filled with God's peace and blessing. But prayer must ever call down this peace upon her walls, gates and stones, and all the servants of the Lord that serve her also. For at the edges of this Jerusalem there is a vulnerability, a divine poverty and exposure, and those who love her must pray for her in her weakness, seeking good for her from God, calling down his peace upon her. And in this work of love, they themselves will find blessing.

O Lord our God, may we ever be glad to go to your house, and in the power of the Spirit find ourselves before your presence, bound in the fellowship of all your worshippers, and renewed by the healing of your judgment and mercy; and grant us ever to persevere in prayer for the well-being of your holy church, the mother who would embrace us all in your new creation.

☙ Psalm 126 ☙

Prayer for the Springing of New Life

1   *When the Lord restored the life of Zion,*
    we were like those who dream.
2   *Then our mouth was filled with laughter,*
    and our tongue with songs of joy.
    Then they said among the nations,
    The Lord has done great things for them.
3   *The Lord indeed did great things for us,*
    and how we then rejoiced!
4   *Restore, O Lord, our life again,*
    as you revive the brooks in the wilderness.
5   *Those who sow with tears*
    shall reap with songs of joy.
6   *One who goes out bitterly weeping, bearing the bag of seed,*
    shall come in singing for joy, bearing the harvest sheaves.

The main point in this fine song is best found in verse 4 – a prayer that the people's exhausted life be renewed. By way of support for this prayer, it is preceded by recollection of past renewal and followed by proverb-style thoughts of suffering turned to joy. The repeated phrase for renewal of life (vv.1a, 4a), the reference to winter rain (v.4b), and to sowing and harvest (v.6) point to the autumn festival as the likely setting.

1–3   The singer beautifully portrays a former happiness resulting from great deeds of the Lord – surely the Lord will desire to give such joy again. In verse 1a we have the phrase traditionally rendered 'turned / brought back the captivity', but now recognized to mean 'turn the turning, restore with a great restoring', virtually 'bring back to life'. The restored people could hardly believe their situation was real (compare Luke 24.41; Acts 12.9).

4   The phrase of verse 1a is used again now in a prayer and clarified for us by a comparison with the wadies of the Negev – gullies running down the arid country on the south of Judah. After the long drought of summer, the winter rains send floods of water down the parched courses, turning them to ribbons of green life. It seems then that the people pray from a death-like situation; their soul cleaves to the dust. Their prayer is for the transforming work of God to restore their life, just as with his rains he brings up grass and flowers in the wilderness.

5–6   The force of the picturesque conclusion may be to express trust in support of the prayer; or it may be that the singer, in prophetic manner, reports to the people his sense of God's favourable response. The 'weeping' and 'rejoicing' have ancient roots in the nature religions and related agricultural customs; but here we have proverbial sayings which declare how weeping or hardship turns to joy as deeds, faithfully done when all seems dead, bear happy fruit.

For a people largely consisting of subsistence farmers and peasants, life and happiness were closely bound up with the annual cycle of growth. The winter rains were vital, but sometimes failed; bondage and starvation then ensued. The psalm's recollection of a time of dream-like joy and the prayer for restoration of life may well relate to good seasons renewing life and joy. The unity of life in land and people was keenly felt. And still today, prayer for new life, for the transformation of dried-up souls and communities to living joy, should also envisage new life and health in earth and waters and a unity of peace among all creatures. The psalm's final assurance has many echoes in the New Testament, which especially tells of a self-giving service, a sowing in death, which brings forth much fruit and finds the great transformation into life eternal (John 12.24f; 1 Corinthians 15.36f).

Lord, as you send rain and flowers even to the wilderness, renew us by your holy Spirit; help us to sow good seed in time of adversity, and so live to rejoice in your good harvest of all creation.

Psalm 127

The Fruitful Sleep

1   If the Lord does not build the house,
    its builders toil on it in vain.
    If the Lord does not guard the city,
    its guard is wakeful all in vain.
2   In vain you rise up early,
    and go so late to your rest,
    eating the bread of anxious toil –
    for he gives to his beloved in sleep.
3   See, children are a heritage bestowed by the Lord;
    the fruit of the womb is given by him.
4   As arrows in the hand of a warrior,
    so are the children born of youthful strength.
5   Happy the one whose quiver he fills with them;
    they shall not be put to shame
      when they speak with adversaries in the gate.

The previous psalm had an ending resembling proverbs, and now we have a song wholly in such Wisdom style. It thus has the form of teaching, but if it were used in a festival, it could suitably testify to the Lord's decisive and generous action in human affairs. It falls into two parts united by the theme of the divine action as decisive.

1–2   The point is made strongly: not just help from the Lord is required as the house is built; it is the Lord himself who must build it. So the toiling builders must be as it were his hands, and their toil only expressive of his. The worshippers might well have thought of the temple and its repair as a prime example. Again, the Lord must not only help guard the city, but actually guard it himself, the watchman serving but as the channel of his work. The singer maintains the striking emphasis as in verse 2 he addresses his people and declares that by their own efforts they can achieve nothing.

However early the rising, however late the taking of rest, however hard the work to produce, without God it is all wasted. 'His beloved', one who trusts in him, is provided for – even while asleep! The thought here is the contrast between an anxious toil which supplants trust, and a life, no doubt dutiful, that rests in the knowledge of the Lord's presence.

3–5 The first word, 'See', indicates that a fresh example will now be given. God's decisive role in human life is now illustrated by the family; children are a heritage and gift that he bestows. Especially in the old Israelite society, children born when mother and father were young became a great support and strength as parents reached middle life. The comparison of the children to arrows and the thought of their value against enemies might suggest that it is the (more literal) 'sons' that are in mind, but old translators were justified in rendering 'children'; the daughters in themselves could prove an immense strength and comfort (Ruth 4.15; Job 42.15) and in marriage might make valuable alliances. The city 'gate' was a complex that included space of social importance; here was much meeting, trading and legal business, and so there were occasions of confrontation with hostile folk. Armed with the children given by the Lord, the parents would not easily be abashed.

The first part of this song beautifully teaches its philosophy of work. Can the house-builder and the city's watchman, with the poet, the singer, and everyone at work, learn to do their work so that the Lord is doing it through them? Can they discover the happiness of work with the soul at peace with God, trusting him a day at a time, waking in the knowledge that he has already provided for the day? Our singer does not mince words; what is done without the Lord is futile, so he says thrice (compare John 15.5).

The second part does not seem spiritually so profound. Granted that it speaks still of God's action, it still seems rather earthy – how those with a big family can stand up to adversaries in the public arena. But it gives a deep appreciation of a fine family: it is seen as a heritage given by the Lord, which under the light of this recognition will be a source of happiness and strength. Later users of the psalm went beyond the concrete case: those who influenced others for good or made disciples for the Lord were indeed blessed with a spiritual family, bringing joy and comfort against adversity. But in any case and above all, the song will leave for everyone who hears its melody, whether or not they have sons or daughters, the mighty teaching of the sleep in God's arms, the resting in his love and care, in trust that he will give and do all that is necessary (similarly Jesus in Matthew 6.25f).

Lord Jesus, who taught us to look at the birds and the raiment of the flowers, we thank you for all you give us as we rest in you; and we pray you to strengthen us by the angels of your love against all adversity.

Psalm 130

Longing and Looking for the Lord

1 Out of the depths, Lord, I call to you;
2 O Lord, listen to my voice.
   May your ears be attentive
   to the sound of my supplications.
3 If you, Lord, retained offences,
   who then, O Lord, could stand?
4 But with you there is forgiveness,
   so that you may be feared.
5 I wait for the Lord, my soul is waiting,
   and for his word I hope.
6 My soul looks for the Lord
       more than watchmen for the morning,
   yes, more than watchmen for the morning.
7 O Israel, wait for the Lord;
   for with the Lord there is faithful love,
       and with him is plenteous redemption,
8 and he will redeem Israel
   from the bonds of all his sins.

With the address to gathered 'Israel' (v.7), this fits well into the series that seems to belong to the great pilgrimage festival of the autumn. In deepest sorrow and penitence, the people are waiting and watching, perhaps at night, looking for the Lord and his word, which was sometimes given at break of morning. The singer is best seen as a representative person, a leading figure who can turn to address and encourage his people. No particular circumstances are revealed in the rather general expressions of the psalm, but we may think the themes well suited to an annual occasion of penitence and expiation.

1–6　The appeal to the Lord rises 'from the depths', the deeps of trouble and affliction. In support of the plea, the singer calls to the Lord as one who does not 'keep' offences, harbouring wrath against the guilty; rather he clears away the sin by forgiveness. This mercy is not to make light of wrongdoing, but to preserve for the Lord a people 'fearing' him, worshipping him, ever mindful of him (Romans 2.4). For without his forgiveness, who would remain? A further consideration urged by the singer is the expectant trust, a hopeful waiting for the Lord. They look for the Lord even more eagerly than watchmen for the sunrise. The comparison may be, as Jewish tradition had it, with the priestly watchers high on the walls, whose duty was to watch for daybreak and give the signal for the first offerings in the temple court.

7–8　The singer now turns to the people and urges them to continue the yearning but trusting watch for the Lord, in sure hope of his faithful love and his abundant 'redemption', his will to save. With prophetic assurance the singer concludes that the Lord will set Israel free from all the bondage that has resulted from sins down the ages.

For all in profound suffering the psalm voices its appeal to the Lord. Conscious of their unworthiness, they are to ground their hope in the forgiving love of God and to watch in penitence, prayer and trust. And in the time of redemption they will tremble at the wonder of the Saviour's love, and live their days in the light of his reality.

Father, we commend to your faithful love those who are crying from the depths; help them to watch and pray through their time of darkness, in sure hope of the dawn of your forgiveness and redemption.

❀❀❀ Psalm 131 ❀❀❀

The Weaned Child upon its Mother

1 Lord, my heart is not haughty, nor my eyes set high;
  I do not concern myself with grand things,
    or matters too marvellous for me.
2 But I have quieted and stilled my soul,
    as a weaned child upon its mother;
  like a weaned child is my soul upon me.
3 O Israel, hope in the Lord,
  from now and for evermore.

Ideas of quietness before the Lord were not restricted to individual spirituality, but could be applied to nations (so 46.10; also 62). This is the case here (v.3). Clearly, the singer has a representative role. He gives the lead in the attitude he describes and can then turn to encourage the festal assembly in such trust. His song may have been inspired in circumstances of hardship for the people, and when little had come from the customary loud laments.

1–2 His address to the Lord leads all the worshippers to take the way of humble trust in seeking relief from present hardships. There was a time for loud cries of protest and even bitter argument with God, a time for giving vent to passionate feelings. But our psalmist has seen that now is a time for humility and restraint. He would pray to God without great demands and arguments; he would acknowledge that God's ways are great and wonderful beyond human understanding. There is much to endure, and his soul might well have clamoured to the Lord. But he has restrained and quietened it, just as a mother soothes and calms a child that makes the transition from breast-feeding; the child has struggled and cried in frustration, until at last it rests peacefully on its mother. The psalmist here sees his soul as a distinct entity that he can talk to and work upon (compare 42.5). So he has brought his soul through to peace and trust, and would let this trust alone be his appeal to the Lord.

3   He concludes his song by directly addressing his people, urging them likewise to wait for the Lord in trustful hope. However long they must wait, let them ever continue, and let them always look to the Lord and believe in his faithfulness.

The Psalms show various aspects of prayer. Like a child they may cry stridently and express their passion; and like a child, so our psalm has it, the Lord's people come humbly to trust in him and quietly wait. For both these kinds of praying comparison with a child has come to mind, and here we find the heart of biblical prayer – a simple turning to the God who is mother and father (compare Matthew 18.2f). But our psalm is an example of prayer without any petition. Its quietness has not been attained easily. Beyond crying and complaining a wonderful rest has been reached, a deep trust that the Lord knows all that is needed and will provide it.

Grant to us, Lord, a quieted and patient spirit, that we may ever hope in you, and wait upon your wisdom and your goodness.

❦ Psalm 137 ❦

Jerusalem Set Above All Joys

1 *By the rivers of Babylon we sat and wept aloud,*
   when we remembered Zion.

2 *On the trees along the banks*
   we hung our lyres unused.

3 *Our captors asked there for a song –*
      those who had despoiled us, for music of joy:
   Sing us one of the songs of Zion.

4 *How should we sing the songs of the Lord*
   on the soil of a foreign land?

5 *If I forget you, O Jerusalem,*
   may my right hand forget its powers.

6 *May my tongue cleave to the roof of my mouth,*
   if I do not remember you,
   if I do not exalt Jerusalem
   above my highest joy.

7 *Remember, Lord, against the people of Edom*
      the day of Jerusalem,
   how they said, Down, down with it, right to its foundations!

8 *O queenly Babylon, great destroyer,*
   happy the one who requites you for all you did to us,

9 *who seizes your children in your turn,*
   and dashes them against the rock.

This passionate poem can be understood as an intercession for Jerusalem in the sorrowful services commemorating the Babylonian destruction of the city, a use found also in later Jewish worship. The psalm begins its prayer by pleading the loyalty to Zion maintained in the Exile (vv.1–4) and now re-affirmed (vv.5–6). The climax is reached with the call for judgement on Jerusalem's murderers – the treacherous Edomites and the ruthless Babylonian conquerors.

1–4   The recollection of the mourning in Babylon may arise from the psalmist's own experience, or from a collective memory preserved in the guild of musicians. The scene is put vividly before the Lord to show the love and loyalty of the worshippers towards his sanctuary. The characteristics of the Babylonian plain, so different to Judah, are well recalled – the great river and its lesser streams and canals, the trees (Euphrates poplars, resembling willows) literally 'in her midst', not in distant woods. The exiles are glimpsed sitting down by the waters, weeping and wailing – an act of mourning, perhaps a formal commemoration (sites by water were favoured for prayer-gatherings, Acts 16.13). The lyres, from which the devoted musicians would not be parted in all their hard journey, were hung silent on the trees in sign of the death-like mourning. The Babylonian captors, asked for the merry music of Zion's festivals. Alas, what an irony there would be in citing the glorious promises to Zion! And how could the holy songs be rightly sung on ground not dedicated to the Lord?

5–6   The singer puts it personally for greatest emphasis as he avows his present devotion. His words are appropriate to a lyrist (v.5b) and a singer (v.6a), and one dedicated to the Lord's service in Zion. He calls a curse upon himself should he ever forget Jerusalem, ceasing to delight in her above his highest joys. His hands could then no longer play and he would never sing again.

7–9   The vow of loyalty has prepared the way for the petition, a call for retributive justice against Jerusalem's destroyers who seem to be going scot-free The neighbouring brother-people of Edom had deserted their allies and indeed assisted the enemy, and had continued to take advantage of Judah's plight. But coming to Babylon's principal share in the outrage, the singer is taken with a prophetic force. He addresses the personified capital city, and pronounces as 'happy' the one who will do to her what she did to Jerusalem, seizing the infants as she had done, and battering them to death against the rock. Not as deadly as the saturation-bombing of modern warfare, the ancient policies of hand-to-hand war were terrible enough. In a case like the Babylonian treatment of repeatedly rebellious Jerusalem, many adults might be spared to serve various purposes for the conquerors, but the infants were killed to end the community's future. The psalmist, from feelings of bitter passion, invokes a justice of retaliation; whoever carries it out, he declares, will have done well.

The first part of the psalm challenges worshippers to profound commitment to the 'Jerusalem' or 'Zion' of their faith – the forms and fellowship which convey the revelation of God. Against this zeal Christians may measure their mindfulness for the church, their setting her above other pleasures, and their consecration of gifts and skills.

But how difficult the use of the concluding imprecations! Some praise the opportunity given here to the powerless to vent their indignation and turn to God for justice; certainly there is evidence here of the dreadful situations through which the biblical faith had to live. Down the centuries, Christians have seen Babylon as an allegory, a symbol of wickedness; her children are our evil thoughts, to be crushed at the outset. Again, some have found value in the prophetic aspect, which can be heard as a warning that evil deeds rebound upon the perpetrators.

In the end, however, the terrible words serve as a reminder that there must always be a discernment of the Spirit in the use of scripture. In the present case the bitter words must at last be washed over by streams of mightier teaching: 'Seek the peace of the city (Babylon) whither I have caused you to be carried away captive, and pray to the Lord for her' (a word of God sent to the exiles, Jeremiah 29.7); 'If your enemy be hungry, give him bread to eat...' (Proverbs 25.2); 'Love your enemies, and pray for those who persecute you...' (Matthew 5.44).

Enable us, Lord, to dedicate our talents and love to the care of your holy church, and grant that in times of her humiliation we may be strong in prayer, both for her restoration and for the repentance and blessing of her adversaries.

Enfolded by God

1   *Lord, you search me and know me.*

2   *You know my sitting and my rising;*
      you discern my thought long before.

3   *You know well my journeying and my halting,*
      and are acquainted with all my paths.

4   *For there is not a word on my tongue,*
      but you, Lord, know it altogether.

5   *Behind and before you enclose me,*
      and lay your hand upon me.

6   *Such knowledge is too wonderful for me,*
      so high that I cannot grasp it.

7   *Where shall I go from your Spirit,*
      or where shall I flee your face?

8   *If I climb up into heaven, you are there;*
      if I make my bed in the depths beneath, you are also there.

9   *If I take the wings of the dawn,*
      and dwell in the farthest sea,

10 *even there your hand shall lead me,*
      and your right hand shall hold me.

11 *If I could say, Let darkness cover me*
      and the light about me turn to night,

12 *even the darkness would not be dark for you;*
      dark and light are alike for you.

13 *It was you that created my inmost parts;*
      you wove me in my mother's womb.

14 *I thank you that I am fearfully and wonderfully made;*
      marvellous are your works, my soul knows well.

15 *My frame was not hidden from you*
         when I was made in secret,
      and wrought in the depths of the earth.

16 *Your eyes saw my form yet unfinished;*
      already my parts were all written in your book.

as day by day they were fashioned,
when not one of them was ready.

17 *How many are your thoughts for me, O God;*
    O how great is the sum of them!

18 *If I count them, they are more in number than the sand;*
    if I reached the end, I would still have you.

19 *O that you would slay the wicked, O God;*
    O that the murderous would go away from me!

20 *For they speak of you with wicked purpose;*
    against you they raise their voice for evil.

21 *Those who oppose you, Lord, do I not oppose,*
    and those who rise against you, do I not abhor?

22 *I oppose them utterly;*
    they have become enemies also for me.

23 *Search me, O God, and know my heart;*
    try me and know my thoughts.

24 *See if there is any hurtful way in me,*
    and lead me in the everlasting way.

The purpose of this distinctive and beautiful psalm is apparent in verse 19 – prayer against murderous men who threaten the psalmist's life. In a long preparation (vv.1–18), he addresses the Lord with praise and thanksgiving, developing especially the theme that his heart and all his ways are known to God. He is thus approaching the Lord with the sincere belief that right is on his side. He invites the scrutiny of this all-knowing God and believes the wicked ones will be found to be God's enemies too. The psalmist may be a king drawing close to God in the sanctuary to gain strength to confront enemies, and so praying in this holy presence with a deep spirituality.

1–12 As is often the case with psalms of supplication, the first word is the holy name. Then, immediately and at length, the supplicant develops the theme of the Lord's searching knowledge of him; God will thus know whether his motives are pure and his cause just. He does not need to assert his integrity directly, but humbly acknowledges that the Lord will know. A tone of praise enters as he describes God's wonderful knowledge of him, a knowledge that constantly embraces all his activity, and too wonderful for him to understand. If he had reason to avoid the divine scrutiny, he could not escape it. In the remotest parts of the cosmos, God would still be with him and about him. And if he could conjure up thick darkness to hide in, it would make no difference; to the divine eye of judgment, the light and darkness are alike.

13–18   The Lord's knowledge of him rests even deeper – not just on God's omnipresence, but also on his role as Creator. The psalmist speaks not of the making of creatures generally, but of his own origin. Beautifully he develops the theme of the Lord's forming, weaving, shaping, intricately working this particular worshipper in his mother's womb, and more mysteriously in the depths of earth, the greater mother (Job 1.21). Thus, beyond even his origin in the womb, back into an ultimate mystery, the Lord knew him and formed destiny for him. For the terrible wonder of it all he must give thanks and praise. Beyond all his reckoning is the weight and abundance of God's thoughts for him; and if he could count them to the end, he would scarcely have begun to comprehend the wonder of God himself.

19–24   The singer's prayer against 'the wicked (man)' and the murderous 'men of blood' is blunt: O that God would kill them and rid him of them! It seems that he refers to particular foes who beset him and threaten his life. He presents them as hostile to God himself, enemies of God's kingdom. The conclusion connects with the beginning of the psalm, as the singer specifically invites God now to search his heart to see if he follows any harmful way. He would be led in the everlasting way ('way of eternity') – granted a continuing life with God.

Troubled by evil adversaries, the psalmist seeks God's help against them. But his prayer is like a meditation, and full of awe. Knowing that his heart must be cleansed, his motives pure, he contemplates the total knowledge that God has of him and all his doings, a knowledge that surrounds in time and space, that sifts, and sees through dark and light, and cannot be evaded in the heights or depths of the universe, a knowledge that is bound up with a loving care and purpose, going back to ultimate origins, continuing in the intricate working and weaving in the womb. What a deep and honest self-searching was needed before this worshipper could call, 'Lord, search me and see if there is any hurtful way in me.' Beyond all the strife of the wicked, he asked to be led on the everlasting way, the path of unbroken communion and life with the Lord.

Church tradition heard here the voice of Christ, but also of every one become part of him. To sing these words sincerely, they also will have searched their own conscience and called upon the Lord's name with awe. They acknowledge him as the reality that closely and always enfolds them, the one of penetrating knowledge, but also of caring thoughts without number for each one. Their prayer against the ruthless is a necessary opposition to his adversaries; but the death they call for is a death to cruel ways and a rebirth in the service of God. And as he leads them on the eternal way, they will at last come to know, even as they are known (1 Corinthians 13.12).

Lord, you know well our journeying and halting, and the sum of your thoughts for us is beyond all our reckoning; help us ever to reject evil and live wholly for you, and lead us in the way everlasting.

Precentors and Priests in the Cosmic Praise

1   Alleluia.
    Praise the Lord from the heavens,
    O praise him in the heights.
2   Praise him, all his angels,
    O praise him, all his hosts.
3   Praise him, sun and moon,
    praise him, all you stars of light.
4   Praise him, heaven of heavens,
    and you waters above the heavens.
5   Let them praise the name of the Lord,
    for he commanded, and they were created.
6   And he established them for ever and ever;
    he gave them a law which they might not transgress.
7   Praise the Lord from the earth,
    you sea-monsters and all ocean depths,
8   fire and hail, snow and mist,
    stormy wind obeying his word,
9   mountains and all hills,
    fruitful trees and all you cedars,
10 you beasts, both wild and tame,
    you creeping things and birds of the air,
11 kings of the earth and all you peoples,
    princes and all rulers of the earth,
12 young men and maidens,
    old people and children together.
13 Let them praise the name of the Lord,
    for his name alone is exalted, his glory over earth and heaven.
14 And he has raised up the horn of his people,
        a cause for praise from all his faithful,
    the children of Israel, a people close to him.

Of psalms which call all creatures into the circle of praise, this is the
most detailed. First, the call to praise goes out to all in the heavens
(vv.1–4), and the grounds are that the Lord created them all by his
word and ensured their continuing functions (vv.5–6). Then the call
is addressed to earth, with her waters, weather, mountains, trees,
animals and peoples in their kinds (vv.7–12), and the grounds are
that his name and glory are exalted over all (v.13). Finally (v.14),
these grounds are developed to include the strength he has given
this people assembled in festal worship at his temple, 'close to him'.
A magnificent counterpart in the late period is found in the
Apocrypha, the Benedicite or Song of the Three Holy Children.

1–6 The singer's call for praise goes first to the heavenly region.
The heavenly beings (angelic servants and fiery hosts), sun, moon,
stars (perhaps especially the planets, visible still in the morning
'light'), the highest heaven itself, and the ocean thought to rest on
heaven's floor, the sky-vault or firmament, are all to sing praise to
the name of the Lord. The grounds for praise are that he created
them, so marvellously too by his word, and through his 'statute' gave
them the way of their happy existence in the harmony of his cosmos.

7–13 The pattern of calls for praise and grounds for praise is now
applied to the earthly region, which also includes the oceans and
great creatures of the waters, and also the atmospheric elements,
where 'fire' may refer to lightning. As to living beings, the singer
calls to the mountains and hills (the main constituents of his
landscape), and to their trees, which will include olives and figs and
the mighty cedars of Lebanon. Each element has its own way of
singing the Creator's praise, and to this great chorus is added the
music of the animals, the reptiles and the birds. People of all
nations, too, are addressed – sturdy young men and women, the
frailer elderly and children; all are summoned to praise the Lord's
'name', his glorious self-revelation, the splendour of his unique
godhead and supremacy over all, the heart of the worshippers'
vision. To behold this glory is reason enough for praise.

14 For the great chorus there is a precentor, a skilled singer who
calls for each contribution. And for the universal host that worships

the holy name there is a central group, a people called to stand close to the Lord and minister for the benefit of all. The psalmist does not distinguish them for a summons of their own, but develops the final grounds for praise to rest at last on the Lord's grace to this people: the raised 'horn', an image from the wild ox, indicates the strength and vitality he has given them; like priests, they are called so to draw near, that they may mediate for all his creatures (Exodus 19.6).

Often in the Psalms we have met the belief that the Creator holds everything that he has made in a relationship to himself, with a commitment of his faithful love. In this relationship all created beings are called to look to him in trust and in praise. In the high moments of worship, when drawing near to the Creator and seeing his glory bring vision of the ideal, this praising universe is real to the pilgrims gathered in the sanctuary. Our psalmist's list of beings who are to sing praise to the name of the Lord may be judged but a slight indication of the innumerable identities in God's cosmos, but it is enough to burst the confines of narrow-minded, imagination-less worship. His vision does not ignore the salvation known in the smaller circle of God's people, indeed this may be taken as its climax. But those brought specially near are led to see the ultimate reach of the Creator's faithful love and the cosmic congregation of his worshippers; they are given his holy strength that they may serve him in this great array, and their praises will only truly delight him when they are reconciled to creatures they have wronged, and so can lead the praises of all in the full sincerity of love.

Almighty Father and Creator, make us so close to you that we grow close to all your creatures, and ready to join in the hymn of all creation, to the praise of your glorious name.

〰 Psalm 150 〰

The Greatest Symphony of All

1 *Alleluia.*
   Praise God in his holy dwelling,
   praise him in the firmament lit with his glory.
2 *Praise him in his mighty acts,*
   praise him in the greatness of his power.
3 *Praise him with the blowing of the trumpet,*
   praise him with the harp and lyre.
4 *Praise him with the drums and dances,*
   praise him with the strings and pipes.
5 *Praise him with the cymbals for proclamation,*
   praise him with the cymbals for acclamation.
6 *Let every living thing*
   praise the Lord. Alleluia.

A concluding hymn, so concise, yet so abundant! Ten main calls to praise are increased to twelve by the opening and concluding alleluias and summarized in the last line with a related word. There are no lines devoted to reasons for praise, but this element is economically covered by the briefest indication of God's glorious appearing and of his might as Creator and Saviour (vv.1–2). Worshippers in the heavenly and earthly temples are summoned to praise; then, with some fullness, the variety of sacred musicians and dancers, and finally all creatures. This colourful poem surely existed first in its own right as a psalm for festal worship, before it came to serve as the Psalter's seal of praise.

1–2 The first call for praise goes out to worshippers in God's sanctuary; to judge from the parallel call (v.1b), this refers primarily to his heavenly dwelling. But with this and its heavenly company, the earthly worshippers readily feel joined. Then the call goes to those in the sky-vault (v.1b), namely sun, moon and starry hosts.

His creatures are to praise him because of his wonderful acts of power and wisdom in creation and beneficent rule.

3–5 Further calls to praise bear more definitely on the worship in the temple courts, envisaging the main resources of the sacred music. The first instrument mentioned, the ram's horn trumpet, was especially used for sacred signals (new moons, sabbaths etc.), but had also an important role in the festal salutations greeting the Lord manifest in glory. In these celebrations, which were mostly processional, the portable harps and lyres carried much of the music. The dancers, especially young women, moved in processional dance with rhythmic tapping of their hand-drums or tambours. The 'strings' may comprehend forms of instruments additional to those of verse 3b, while the 'pipes' may be a kind of flute or be intended comprehensively for the woodwind. The two kinds of cymbals are those for 'proclamation' (literally 'hearing', in festal worship perhaps in proclamations like 'The Lord is King') and for 'acclamation' (greeting the victorious Lord). The combination of such instruments is noted in the festal procession of 2 Samuel 6.5.

6 In keeping with the psalm's economy of wording, the summarizing conclusion says much in few words. Much indeed, for it summons every 'breath', meaning every creature given life by God, to praise him. Concluding a psalm that has addressed all in the heavens and in the temple, symbolic centre of the universe, this last summons will be meant with all the scope of Psalms 98 and 148. Every being in which the Creator has breathed his life is to direct that life to him, rejoicing to know and behold him, to trust him, to honour his will, to testify to him and to exalt him above all else. The final alleluia ('Praise ye Yah') appropriately ends all with its short form of the name 'Yahweh', 'He That Only Is'. God the Creator, so utterly beyond the understanding of creatures, has given himself to them in grace to be known as their constant guide and helper, ever present to them in the name above all names.

So terse, this last of the psalms, and yet with more words than any other for the musical instruments! Enveloped in references to God's servants in the heavens and to every being in his cosmos, the musicians and dancers here will have a representative role. At the heart of the worship before God's face, they represent every voice in earth, seas and heavens. As horns are blown, frame-drums tapped, strings swept and plucked, pipes breathed and cymbals shivered, the sounds of nature come together – the praise of the waters and the winds, grasses and leaves, lions and birds, goats and oxen, mothers and children, and the circling, turning dancers represent the movement of the world round God, from him and to him again.

But this scene of highest joy is not characteristic of all the ancient worship; it was not a standard procedure whenever people gathered in God's name. The dramatic course of the festival, itself reached by a hard pilgrimage, passed through penitential abasement, depths of fear and sorrow, vigils of silence and hope, before such joy prevailed. In the Psalter itself, our ecstatic psalm stands at the end of a long story of tears and complainings, outnumbering the praises. But still it stands as the final testimony. Through all the pain and conflict, by the way of humility, trust and hope, of prayer and praise, the open gates are found, inviting to the cosmic celebration before the face of the one who at last has made all well in peace and love.

Almighty and gracious Lord, lead us through all doubts and sufferings into the world lit by your glory, that we may join with full heart in the music of all your creatures, in praise and thanksgiving to your holy name.

∽ *Index* ∽

(with themes for meditation)